Opportunity Knocks

Open the Door to
an Extraordinary Life

Pat Mesiti

© Pat Mesiti Ministries Inc. 2001
  PO Box 6873, Baulkham Hills Business Centre
  NSW Australia 2153
  pat@mesiti.com

Educational, motivational, leadership

ISBN 0-9587336-1-9

Cover design by Chris Perry Graphic Design

Book design by Kingsclear Books (+61) 02 9439 5093
kingsclear@wr.com.au
PO Box 335 Alexandria
Australia 1435

Printed by Griffin Press

CONTENTS

Dedication
To my faithful staff at Teen Challenge,
New South Wales. Their commitment and tireless
efforts are an inspiration. And also to the young men
who have taken the opportunity to break the power
of life-controlling habits. Their courage and
determination to overcome
makes them heroes over those
who choose to quit.

Thanks

*I would like to thank Graeme Kirkwood,
Jeremy Horn, Craig Heilmann and Mark Badham
for their assistance with this book.
Thanks also to Lisa Sylvester,
my Personal Assistant,
for her long hours,
hard work and
gentleness of spirit.*

INTRODUCTION

Grab Opportunities and Wring Success Out of Them!

Why is it that some people recognise opportunities and others don't? It seems that successful people around us manage to grab opportunities out of thin air and wring success out of them. If you are one of those millions of people around the world who are waiting for an opportunity to take your life to another level, then this book is for you. This book will help you understand the elements of opportunity so that you can achieve the greatest potential from it.

Opportunities come our way in various forms and sizes and often they are disguised. Most opportunities are "slippery little suckers", as Julia Roberts said in the movie *Pretty Woman*.

We've all faced opportunities in the past, from choosing school subjects and career paths, to life partners and business associates. In fact, opportunities are staring at you right now, and will continue to challenge you into the future. No period of time in history holds a mortgage on opportunity: it exists in the past, present and future. And opportunity comes to us all.

The 21st century will offer you many new opportunities. The new millennium, still in its infancy, holds a vast amount of opportunity for a wider audience than ever before. The early years of this century will determine whether you and your family progress and prosper or whether you become less than effective and, as a result, non-achievers. If you fall into the latter category, you will surely fail to gain the prosperity you desire and deserve.

This book deals with the opportunities that come across our paths. How you handle these opportunities will determine your success or failure. How you handle lost opportunities, for instance, may well be the key to your future. If you want to get the most out of the opportunities that come your way, you must know what to do when you see one; in fact, you really need to know what an opportunity looks like. Quite often they come surprise-packaged in the gift-wrapping of something else.

Opportunity knocks. Can you hear it? If you can't first hear it, you won't open it … and it will move on.

I believe it was Milton Berle who once said, "If opportunity doesn't knock, build a door". A door provides an opportunity to us, that we may walk through it to a new phase in life, a new environment and a magnificent future.

Many people approach doors timidly. Others walk right through them. People in the former group wait for an opportunity to knock, but they don't actually have a personal door to knock on. Very often

> "If opportunity doesn't knock, build a door."
> Milton Berle

these same people have instead built walls – preconceptions about what an opportunity looks like. For example, if a secretary refuses to take the opportunity to learn computer skills because she has always used a typewriter, her wall of resistance and preconception – because she's "always done it that way" – will hold her back from many opportunities for future employment.

However, to grasp the new opportunities that will come your way, you must create a new mindset within yourself and within the generations that will follow you. You must develop a willingness to take risks, to find new ways of putting your dreams into motion, and to challenging the nine-to-five mentality that leaves us prisoners to debt. If you develop such a mindset, where time becomes a friend rather than a foe, you are heading down the path to success.

CHAPTER ONE

What Does an Opportunity Look Like?

*The world is filled with unfortunate souls who didn't hear
opportunities knock at the door, because they were down
at the convenience store buying lottery tickets.*

Napoleon Hill

How often in life have we noticed someone else
achieving great success, financial wealth and a great
lifestyle and called it luck? How often have we faced
opportunities to create something better for ourselves,
but rejected the opportunity we were given, simply
because it didn't look like an opportunity? (In fact,
opportunity often looks more like a challenge.) When
someone else capitalizes and prospers on the opportu-

nity we passed over, we have the gall to call them 'lucky'. Opportunities get handed to us, but it is up to us to make them a reality. They don't simply happen by themselves.

More often than not, opportunities come disguised as problems. Chuck Swindoll has wisely observed, "We are all faced with a series of great opportunities, brilliantly disguised as impossible situations." How true that simple statement is. Opportunity rarely ever comes emblazoned with a flashing neon sign. I have heard it said that the bigger the opportunity the faster it moves. Our attitude towards that fast moving opportunity will determine whether we capitalize on it and make something happen, or whether it passes us by, and let someone else take hold of it.

When Decca Records knocked back the opportunity to sign the Beatles, because they didn't like "their sound", they failed to capitalize on the fast-moving opportunity that had come to them. These four Liverpool rockers swept the world, set attendance records, are arguably the greatest rock-and-roll band of all time, and their songs have been indelibly imprinted on the minds and hearts of generations.

> *"We are all faced with a series of great opportunities, brilliantly disguised as impossible situations"*
> *Chuck Swindoll*

Let's do a little exercise: finish these musical lines from some Beatles songs:

"She loves you..."

"I wanna hold your...."

"We all live in a...."

"Can't buy me...."

"Let it...."

"Hey...."

Get the picture! Yet, Decca Records let it all slip through their fingers. The genius that bypassed the opportunity cost his company hundreds of millions of dollars. With hindsight, we could say, "How stupid! I would have grabbed that opportunity?" Would you? It neither looked nor sounded like an opportunity – just four scruffy lads from the back streets of Liverpool with no hope and no obvious future – at least to some.

Consider Colonel Sanders. In fact, consider the 2060 knock-backs of his secret recipe for chicken. Finally, on the 2061st knock-back, someone took a shot at the moving target, opened the door, and hit the chicken in the tail. Along with those scattered feathers came billions of dollars, as literally millions of chickens have laid down their lives to keep the Colonel's dream alive. (I believe most chickens are born destined to fulfil the Colonel's grand vision, and so did he!)

Opportunities are not luck; they are taken. Opportunities

Opportunities are not luck; they are taken.

almost always look irrelevant. They often look insignificant, small and, frequently, challenging. The giant oak tree grows from a tiny acorn; however, you have to first get an acorn. The potential of its greatness lies in that acorn. Consider an apple. You can count the apple seeds in an apple, but you cannot count the apples in an apple seed. The lesson, friends, is that the opportunity before you

> *The giant oak tree grows from a tiny acorn; the potential of its greatness lies in that acorn.*

may not seem great now, but in the future it can become like a huge tree brimming with fruit.

When I began our nationally recognised youth organisation, Youth Alive, in New South Wales (Australia), it did not look like a great opportunity; it looked like a mess. What began as an insignificant handful of teenagers has exploded to the point where more than 11,000 young people attended one meeting. Youth Alive now sees venues filled to capacity wherever it holds events throughout my home state of New South Wales. That opportunity didn't look anything like it does today. There were no leaders, very few musicians, no resources, no financial support, and only the seed of a dream.

Just recently, I had another opportunity to take over a drug recovery program, which, to put it mildly, was a disaster. It definitely didn't look like an opportunity; it looked like one massive headache. But it was in fact an opportunity, cleverly disguised as a complete mess.

Today, the program is flourishing: adult men are being rehabilitated; the homeless are being housed; people are supporting it financially and with their time and skills. Why? They now see an opportunity – not an acorn, but an oak tree. Seventy-six young men have been through the program in 18 months and are on their way to a drug free life – their nightmares have been replaced by dreams.

If you take an opportunity when it's an acorn, people will brag about what a great tree-grower you are. Famous US statesman, politician, jurist and humanitarian James F. Byrnes once said, "Too many people are thinking of security instead of opportunity."

> *"Too many people are thinking of security instead of opportunity."*
> *James F. Byrnes*

It is my experience that there are at least six key signs that will reveal that what you may have before you is an opportunity rather than a problem. To recognize an opportunity, you will have to:

1. See the end, not the beginning.
2. Get an opportunist's mindset.
3. Avoid looking for an easy way.
4. Be prepared for your day of opportunity – because it's disguised as today!
5. Make the most of every circumstance.
6. Grasp it with both hands – i.e., wholeheartedly and passionately.

Let's see how these six vital signs of opportunity stack up in real life.

See the End, Not the Beginning

Opportunities are based on chance and choice: when you get a chance, make the choice! In other words, when opportunity knocks, you must choose whether to let it come in. The ball is in your court. Dr Maxwell Maltz, in *The Search for Self Respect*, says, "You create opportunity. You develop the capacities for moving toward opportunities. You turn crises into creative opportunities, and defeats into successes, and frustration into fulfilment."

The first key, then, to recognizing opportunities is to believe that only you decide what is a problem and what is an opportunity. How you respond to circumstances determines whether they become opportunities to advance yourself, your career, and your lifestyle. But we must initiate and not procrastinate when we see the potential in an opportunity. We must have a sense of adventure rather than intimidation. Human nature tends to first react with intimidation rather than with adventure; intimidation's primary role is to rob you of opportunity.

> *"You create opportunity. You turn crises into creative opportunities, and defeats into successes, and frustration into fulfilment."*
> Dr Maxwell Maltz

However, if you perceive any challenge as an adventurous process in which you can learn and grow and thrive, then you will be in an advantageous mindset to turn obstacles into opportunities. Let me illustrate this for you. Someone may come to you with a brand new business opportunity. It requires time, effort and resources. In other words, there is an element of cost. What is your first response? Probably to get intimidated by the costs! Next you find people around you who will confirm your worst fears. (We can always find experts lacking experience who will reinforce our intimidating fears.) Eventually, you will be turned against the very opportunity by which you might attain freedom, financial security, and many other benefits.

This happens in many areas of life, such as marriage or raising children. People often say, "Be careful of the terrible twos". Others say, "How difficult it is to raise children in such a negative environment" or "The teenage years are a nightmare full of rebellion and problems, and then, when they get married and leave home, your kids never think of you or visit; they are too busy for mum and dad, who did so much for them." Let me ask you: with this kind of mindset, at what point does raising children ever become a joy?

I have found that bringing up children is a challenge, but not a nightmare. Sure, at two years of age, crawling into cupboards and pulling out the pots and pans, it's hard to see the latent opportunity, but at least your kids are developing musical talent! As teenagers your children will struggle with authority and independence, but you are bringing up an adult; it's an opportunity to mould, teach and train. I've found that bringing up children is fantastic. There may be ups and downs, but that's the process of growth. It's an opportunity to invest in the future.

Apart from speaking to the corporate sector and training and mobilizing people, I oversee two of the most effective youth programs in the world. We regularly face difficult situations with teens. However, I don't see the problems; I see the incredible opportunities in the potential these young people

If you look for opportunity, you will find it everywhere. You determine opportunity.

have. They are acorns that will grow into oaks; they can turn their tragedies into triumphs. Let me put it to you simply: where you stand determines what you see. If you look for opportunity, you will find it everywhere. *You determine opportunity.*

Get an Opportunist's Mindset

The second rule to recognizing an opportunity is your circumstance. With opportunity it is possible to conceive how, through a systematic plan and the right attitude, you can benefit from your circumstances. Find the win in any situation and you have found an opportunity. In other words, if *you determine* the difference between opportunity and problem, then anything can have a win in it – every cloud can have a silver lining. Opportunities come, and they may not be our preferred option, but the win is found in taking advantage of every situation to enhance your own experience.

Motivational writer O.S. Marden has said, "There is power lying latent everywhere, waiting for the observant eye to discover it." I recently read that in 1948, Gene Autry was looking for a Christmas song to match the success of his popular 1947 song, *Here Comes Santa Claus*. Apparently Autry wanted to cut two records and needed four songs, but he only had three. Around that time a young New York songwriter sent him the lyrics and music for *Rudolph the Red Nosed Reindeer*. Autry thought the song silly, but his wife loved it. In the final recording session he recorded the song. That simple song, which Autry almost discarded, went on to sell two-and-a-half million copies that year alone. Since then, *Rudolph* has been recorded by over 400 artists in almost every language and has sold in excess of 100 million copies. That's what I call seeing the win. He didn't see it, but his wife did. How many times does this happen every day?

> "There is power lying latent everywhere, waiting for the observant eye to discover it."
> O.S. Marsden

Inventor, Thomas Edison, has this story, told by his son, to illustrate what I am saying about seeing the win. Edison's entire laboratory, experiments and research one day burst into flames. His son Charles, concerned for his father's well-being, immediately rushed to his side, worrying that his father would be in torment and grief for all his research, study and experiments. "Quick," said his father, "go and get your mother!" Charles Edison wondered why he should do that. When he asked why, the old inventor said, "Tell her to hurry, she'll never see a fire this big again." But that's not the end of the story. The next day as Edison walked through the ashes and rubble, he began to say with great excitement, "Thank God! Thank God! The world will never know all of my mistakes and failures; they are burnt and gone forever." That's seeing the win!

Assuming you encounter a challenge on your way to fame, as Edison did, and you face rejection, loss, an up-hill climb, will you see the win in the cost? Or will you only see the loss? Every day, opportunity cries out to us, but like I said, it is often disguised. It is up to you to recognize it as opportunity.

Imagine for a moment that someone came to you and said that you have the potential to start your own business, that you could make money from it, and that they'd show you how. What would go through your mind? You might count the cost: time, effort, hard work on top of your regular job, sacrifices etc. but, you might also look for the win: extra income, friendships, and personal growth.

Avoid Looking for an Easy Way
The third key is to see in every circumstance the potential to fulfil your life vision. Opportunity is always a gift that creates for us the chance to be above not beneath, the head not the tail, victorious and not defeated.

But opportunities will not always be easy to handle. So don't look for the easy way with an opportunity, go with the hard way! Too many people think an opportunity should simply drop in their lap, but opportunities are shaped and created by the ways in which we approach them. You will never – I repeat NEVER – fulfil your life vision if you go the easy way.

> *"Two roads diverged in a wood, and I took the one less traveled by, And that has made all the difference."*
> *Robert Frost*

Dream big dreams for yourself and go the difficult route. American poet, Robert Frost, so aptly put it in his well-known poem *The Road Not Taken*:

> *Two roads diverged in a yellow wood,*
> *And sorry I could not travel both*
> *And be one traveler, long I stood*
> *And looked down one as far as I could*
> *To where it bent in the undergrowth;*
> *Then took the other, as just as fair…*

The poem ends with:

> *Two roads diverged in a wood, and I -*
> *I took the one less traveled by,*
> *And that has made all the difference.*

Don't go the road that all the punters are going – because you'll glean the same results as them!

Be Prepared for Your Day of Opportunity

Your opportunity day is today. There is no shortage of opportunities in the world; only a shortage of opportunists – people who are ready with both hands to grab the opportunities that come their way. I once heard a motivational speaker make a very telling point: while every day, billions of people around the planet sit crying over their soup bowls, saying no good thing ever came their way – trillions of dollars of economic activity literally zap and zoom around the planet. If you want some of those dollars, the speaker said, all you have to do is stick your hand out

> *There is no shortage of opportunities in the world; only a shortage of opportunists.*

and grab them. And he's right! Today is your day of opportunity!

Make the Most of Every Circumstance

Joni Erikson-Tada was confined to a wheelchair through a tragic accident. In the midst of her pain and suffering, she began to develop the skill of painting using only a brush held in her teeth. Now, each year she speaks to literally thousands of people, giving them hope in the midst of their pain – all because she sees opportunity as a gift through which we may become what we are destined to be.

Successful people have a way of capitalizing on opportunities, to shape them and to form them into a gift that can benefit themselves and others. That's the beauty of opportunity. Disguised as hardship, nuisance and pain, as it so often is, it becomes opportunity when we approach it from the right angle.

Helen Keller, who was asked what could be worse than being blind, said, "Being able to see, but having no vision". Do you think that statement would be as powerful if she had physical sight? She sees the circumstance of her blindness as a gift to become a better person.

Grasp Your Opportunity with Both Hands

Opportunities wait for no one. You must be diligent, circumspect and eager. Grasp the opportunities that come your way! Make them your own and run with them. Opportunity is everywhere, but it's up to you to grab an opportunity when you see it.

In this chapter, I have outlined the six keys for identifying an opportunity. I hope I have convinced you that anything can be an opportunity. No circumstance in which you find yourself needs to be a problem; on the contrary, if responded to correctly, every situation has supernatural potential latent within it. The key is your attitude (and response); whether you see a win in it and are prepared to do the hard yards. The key is to recognize the gift nature of opportunity: that opportunities exist today and that it is up to you to grab them! You have 'gifted' opportunities in life,

Don't wait for the boat to dock - make a 'splash' by swimming out to meet it.

and it is up to you to choose to make them work for you.

Now is the opportune time for anything. Things happen at 'opportune' moments – not necessarily at convenient moments. If you wait for the right time, the perfect setting, the right feeling, when all the pieces are in place – you'll still be waiting this time next century. Opportunity will pass you by. Don't wait for the boat to dock – make a 'splash' by swimming out to meet it.

CHAPTER TWO

Myths about Opportunity

Opportunism is the practice of taking advantage of any opportunity to gain money or power for yourself.

Collins Australian Dictionary

When you first read the above quote, you could be tempted to see it in a negative light – that opportunism is somehow something devious, underhanded, sneaky and to be viewed with suspicion. When I read the quote, I see opportunism and opportunity as a means to create a more meaningful, prosperous and influential life, for others and myself.

There is nothing wrong with wanting to gain more money or power – these things in themselves are not good or bad. Power, money, influence and success take on the characteristics of the people who have them.

We should place opportunities and a sense of opportunism into the hands of good people, with fair-minded intentions, who desire to be a good influence, rather than allowing money, power, influence, wealth and creativity to fall into the hands of the wrong people.

There are five myths about opportunity I will outline in this chapter. These simple misunderstandings tempt us away from opportunities to create success for ourselves. By having and maintaining an inadequate view of opportunities, we cheat ourselves and miss out on many good things that could be ours.

The Moral Bankruptcy Argument

You Must Be Doing It Wrong

The first of these myths about opportunity is that *if you take up an opportunity, you are somehow perceived to be morally bankrupt.* This is obviously not the case. How you use your opportunities, however, will reflect the type and quality of person you are. The failure to take opportunities is far more serious than actually taking them, provided, of course, that the opportunities we take are good, productive and helpful. Not taking such opportunities may be seen as laziness or disinterest.

> *Dietrich Bonhoffer wrote that for evil men to triumph, all good people have to do is ... nothing!*

It seems to me morally wrong for good people not to

take opportunities for money, power and influence. Dietrich Bonhoeffer wrote that for evil men to triumph, all good people have to do is ... nothing!

In 415 BC, the Greek historian, Thucydides, wrote, "Wealth to us is not a mere material for vainglory but an opportunity for achievement, and poverty – we think it no disgrace to acknowledge but a real degradation to make no effort to overcome". Let me say it in plain 21st-century language: people find it easier to put down wealth and affluence instead of helping others to get out of circumstances of poverty and hardship. It's easy to criticize the wealthy, but the rich, by being opportunists, generally create opportunities for themselves and others to overcome poverty.

> *"Wealth to us is not a mere material for vainglory but an opportunity for achievement ..."*
> Thucydides

Bill Gates III, for example, is a very wealthy man. How many other people has he made wealthy or employed, and how many other businesses have benefited and derived opportunities from Microsoft products and/or its associated companies? Literally hundreds of thousands! Try imagining today's life without *Windows!*

Opportunity Discriminates

This leads me to the second myth, that somehow *opportunity is discriminating in whom it chooses to bless.*

We talk about these people as being 'lucky'. I love this quote: "Success is a matter of luck; ask any failure!" In fact, opportunity is no respecter of persons; it respects principles, such as making the most of circumstances!

Samuel Goldwin, the film and media mogul, once said, "I think luck is the essence to recognise an opportunity and the ability to take advantage of it. Everyone has had breaks, but everyone also has opportunities. The man who can smile at his breaks and grab his chances [opportunities] gets on." Oprah Winfrey says it more succinctly but with equally force, "Luck is a matter of preparation meeting opportunity".

In our modern world, people are waiting for their boat to come in – the lottery ticket, the 'sure thing' at the track, an inheritance through a hated old aunt who dies suddenly and precipitously (and mysteriously after you cooked for her!) in her sleep. But did you know that according to the best-selling book, *The Millionaire Next Door*, 80 percent

> *"I think luck is the essence to recognise an opportunity and the ability to take advantage of it"*
> Samuel Goldwin

of America's millionaires are first-generation rich; two-thirds are self-employed. They did not inherit opportunity; they created it. They do not feel sorry for themselves for not being born 'successful'; they merely change their circumstances through positive action. Do you get the point!

Opportunity is Perpetual

The third myth about opportunity is that *my opportunity will always be there*. No opportunity is ever permanent. I catch planes on a weekly basis. Upon arrival at the airport I am issued a boarding pass, which gives me the opportunity to catch my plane. The airline generally issues a boarding call, but if I fail to board, the airline usually gives both a final and then a personal boarding call. If the plane is due to leave at 10.00 am, but I don't board within ten minutes or so of that time, the airline will generally release my seat to another passenger on standby, waiting for his or her opportunity to board. Not only will I miss my flight, missing it will throw into chaos my day, my plans and my life! All because I thought I could board at any time, at my leisure. That is a huge mistake. King Solomon said, "Time and chance happen to us all". Make sure that when it's your time, you take your chance.

Eighty percent of America's millionaires are first-generation rich; two-thirds are self-employed. They did not inherit opportunity; they created it.

Opportunity makes itself available to you: if you don't take it, somebody else will. Now is the time to make the most of opportunities – not next week or next year. "Opportunities are never lost," an anonymous saying goes, "The other fellow takes those you miss". Opportunity sits around waiting for no-one. It moves on.

Past Failure Prevents Opportunity

Turning Disadvantage to Advantage

The fourth myth about opportunity is that *today's great opportunity is hindered or robbed by yesterday's failures*. In fact, today is a new day! Let me give you an example. My good friend and renowned South African speaker, Andre Olivier, has written about Charles Steinmetz, whom he calls "an electrical genius":

> He [Steinmetz] *one of the founding fathers of the colossal General Electric, was crippled from birth. His body was grotesque; he was so short in stature that he looked like a dwarf; he was a hunchback.*
>
> *His mother died before he was one-year-old. His father was comparatively poor, but was determined that as far as possible, young Charles would have a thorough education. He could not play normal games as other boys did, so he decided to devote himself to science. His theme of life was "I will make discoveries that will help other people".*
>
> *When he migrated to the United States, he could not speak a word of English. His face was swollen from the cold he endured on the trip; his sight defective; his dwarf stature and misshapen body coupled with shabby dress tempted Port authorities to return him to Switzerland. Charles stayed; he got an oppor-*

tunity to work a $12-dollar-a-week job. The infant company that employed him, called General Electric, realized that they had a genius, an expert in the field of electricity. His career was marked by research and development that even to this day inspires many. When he died in 1923, they said, "This deformed hunchback had the mind of an angel and the soul of a seer."

This story illustrates how failures, physical handicaps or emotional struggles should never stop us from grabbing opportunities and making a better tomorrow. Tragic pasts make great testimonials for the future.

From Slavery to Freedom

In his book, *Will Daylight Come?*, Robert Heffler tells the following moving story. There was a little boy out playing in the woods. He had been given a slingshot, but he could never hit his intended targets. As he was walking home, he swung his slingshot and accidentally killed his grandmother's duck. He was greatly disturbed, so he hid the duck, but then he noticed that his sister had seen everything. She remained silent. Later, their grandmother asked his sister to do the dishes. His sister said, "Johnny wants to do

The tendency of human nature is to enslave us to our past fears, failures and problems, rather than to launch out to new opportunities.

the dishes." She then whispered to Johnny, "Remember the duck!" The next day their grandfather asked them to go fishing, but grandmother said, "I need someone to help me with supper!" The boy's sister declared, "Oh, Johnny would like to do that," and she whispered, "Remember the duck!" Then she went fishing. After a week of torment, Johnny confessed to his grandmother, and she said, "I know. I saw everything. I forgive you. I was just wondering how long you'd let your sister make you a slave to your past."

The tendency of human nature is to enslave us to our past fears, failures and problems, rather than allowing us to be freed, and to launch out to new opportunities. Perhaps in the past we have suffered rejection, so getting involved in a new business venture that involves taking a bold step raises fears. I know many people in the business world who, through fear of rejection, have carried their fears of that into the present, and missed the opportunities that could have propelled them into an incredible future.

No Hard Work

The fifth myth about opportunity is that *successful people replace skill and hard work with opportunism*, when in fact the opposite is true. An old saying goes, "The harder I work, the luckier I get!"

There is a story told of an art lover who watched the great Picasso paint a picture in a matter of a few hours. The art lover

> *An old saying goes, "The harder I work, the luckier I get!"*

commented how great it must be to be able to paint a painting and create something that is a masterpiece in such a short period of time. Picasso replied, "You weren't there to watch the 40 years of work that went into my art."

Opportunism Never Replaces Skill and Diligence

I am an avid fan of Italian soccer. Because I'm an Italian fan, I am going to take this opportunity to say that Italian soccer is the best in the world. Everybody in Italy is an expert – from the sidelines! In the last World Cup, a young Australian-Italian, called Christian Vieri, stormed onto the world stage by continually scoring goals. One of my friends, an Italian of course, said to me, "Vieri is not a great player; he's just an opportunist!" What a stupid thing to say!

Let me get this straight: the whole idea of the game of soccer is to kick the ball past the defence, while overcoming tackles, avoiding the off-side trap, and while running at unbelievable speed, in front of 100,000 people and millions watching on TV, followed by a lynch-mob in the Italian sports media, finally putting the ball with pin-point accuracy past the goalkeeper and into your opponent's net. I thought this was the whole idea – to score goals! Apparently, according to my friend, it isn't.

If Christian Vieri listened to the bantering of people such as my friend, when the ball is passed to him and he has an opportunity to score, he would ask himself, "What will people think?" and graciously return the ball to the opposition, and then apologize for the inconvenience of making them run to him to get the ball! Why? He doesn't want to be an opportunist! Let's be serious, shall we? The whole idea is to seize your opportunity and make it count.

You can apply these principles to sports, business and life. The good Book says, "As we have opportunity, let us do good ... ".

Opportunities come and will continue to come, if we make the most of them. If Christian Vieri got the ball and did not score or attempt to score, he wouldn't last in the game. That is why many people in the game of life fail to win – they don't take advantage of their opportunities.

> *The opportunist takes the opportunity, makes the most of the opportunity and gets given more opportunities.*

We all know that marriage, like all relationships, has its struggles. However, when opportunity arises to romance, to give a gift, to give a word of encouragement to your partner or spouse, if you have the idea that your partner or spouse will perceive you as an opportunist, you will never build an open and caring relationship. Here's the difference between those who are accused of being opportunistic and the spectators who wait for it all to happen – the opportunist takes the opportunity, makes the most of the opportunity and gets given more opportunities, while the spectator just criticizes from the lounge chair.

All these myths will rob you of opportunity. Take

the initiative. It's not a matter of luck. Remaining crippled by your past or having fear of being perceived as an opportunist will make you unsuccessful, but avoiding the myths, taking the initiative and capitalizing on your opportunities will bring you success. In the words of Dave Thomas, founder of Wendy's, "A little initiative will improve your luck nine days out of ten".

Just remember, people who hang on to myths rarely embrace opportunities.

CHAPTER THREE

The Elements of Opportunity

*Many do with opportunities as children do
at the seashore. They fill their little hands with sand,
and then let the grains fall through one by
one, until they're all gone.*

Thomas Jones

Rita Coolidge has rightly said: "Too often, opportunity knocks, but by the time you push back the chain, push back the bolt, unhook the two locks and shut off the burglar alarms, it's too late." The motto is "be like the boy scouts" – be prepared!

Being prepared is a key factor to making the most of opportunities. It is easy to forget how important preparation is. Here, the visionary boat-builder, known to us as Noah, should be our guide. Remember, it wasn't raining when Noah built the ark. In fact he was prepared, in spite of not even knowing what rain was. (Some would say Noah was blessed in being blissfully ignorant of what rain was – he had no preconceptions or fears.)

Preparation will help you to be ready for opportunity when it comes; rather than being preoccupied by preconceptions of what opportunity is or isn't, you'll be productive.

When I received my first opportunity to speak, some 20 years ago, I was prepared. I didn't have time to think, "This is not really what I'm looking for," simply because it wasn't as large as I envisioned my future to be. I took it. More recently, I spoke to an audience of 60,000 people in the United States of America. I was so good, I bought my own tapes and books! This did not just happen; I've been in preparation for today's opportunities all my life. Yesterday, I was making myself ready.

"Too often, opportunity knocks, but by the time you push back the chain, push back the bolt, unhook the two locks and shut off the burglar alarms, it's too late."
Rita Coolidge

In this chapter, we will consider the elements – the key factors – that will help us make the most of the opportunities that knock on our doors. These factors are not exhaustive, though you will find that many are essential to making the most of your opportunities.

Making the Most of Time

Live Like a Champion

The first element to grasping opportunities is making the most of time. Champion boxer, Muhammad Ali, said this: "I hated every minute of the training, but I said, 'Don't quit. Suffer now and live the rest of your life as a champion!'" Many people want instant fulfilment or gratification. Instant gratification generally lasts as long as the gratifying event; it's short term. Rare is the overnight success, the instant millions – as quickly as these come, they go.

I was working in my garden recently and one of my interns was working with me. As we stopped for a brief drink, he looked at me, with my shovel in my hand, and asked, "Pat, when does serving stop? When can I do what you do?" I'm sure if I'd decapitated him that day, God would have quickly forgiven me. He seemed to think that everything came instantly. Too often we look at successful people and say, "That's what I want to be!" We see the snapshot of the now. What we should see is the movie of the whole life! This takes time.

> "I hated every minute of the training, but I said, 'Don't quit. Suffer now and live the rest of your life as a champion!' "
> Muhammad Ali

It takes time to grow. It takes time to prepare. It

takes time to learn. It also takes time to reach the next stage, to win the race. We must remember that success is a marathon, not a sprint. Time tests and proves what we really are. Over time the cream always rises to the top.

> *Success is a marathon, not a sprint. Time tests and proves what we really are.*

Time affects different things in different ways. For instance, time affects milk in a certain way (just go to your fridge and check!) and wine in another. The common element is time, but the reaction is determined by the make-up of the products.

A Tale of Three Men

Let me illustrate. In 1945, three outstanding and gifted speakers thundered across America. Have you ever heard of Chuck Templeton? How about Brian Clifford? Does Billy Graham ring any bells?

All three contemporary speakers were gifted, eloquent and powerful. It was said of Templeton that he was the most gifted and talented preacher in America. "He would be the next Babe Ruth in the Church", trumpeted an influential magazine. It was said of Clifford that he was the most powerful speaker in centuries; people lined up outside auditoriums ten deep, and 12 hours before his scheduled appearance, just to hear him speak. In 1945, at Baylor University, the president ordered the bells to be turned off, so that Clifford could speak without interruption. He spoke for two hours and 15 minutes and kept the audience spellbound. He touched more lives, influenced more leaders and set more attendance records than any man in his day. He was even offered a movie role in *The Robe*. Billy Graham, by contrast, was almost ignored and was simply called "puffing Billy".

By 1950, just five years later, Templeton abandoned the ministry for radio and TV work. By 1954, Clifford lost his family, his health and his life. Alcohol had destroyed him. At 35 years of age, he was found dead in a run-down hotel room in Amarillo, Texas. Within ten short years, only one of the three still had his life on track, and Billy

> *Be faithful with the little opportunities that come and prove ourselves worthy of greater opportunities.*

Graham, regardless of religious, political or social background, is consistently noted as one of the most influential and honourable men of all time. Time will tell how you respond to challenges, problems and opportunity. What's inside you will come out over time.

Success takes time, so we should be faithful with the little opportunities that come and prove ourselves worthy of greater opportunities.

Focus

The second element is *focus*. What is focus? If you consider many of history's great people, you will find that they were known for what they focused on. In other words, what you give your attention to.

Isn't it amazing that some people start life with just a few pennies in their bank, and go on to build incredible wealth because they give it attention. Other people can start out with huge amounts of money, perhaps an inheritance, yet over time, because they don't give it attention, they squander their wealth. What you pay attention to will cause you to progress.

Priority Doesn't Happen by Chance, but by Choice
Similarly, what you pay attention to becomes your priority. We choose our priorities. We have to choose each day to pursue our opportunity. In 1999, I had the privilege of being at an event with prominent Australian performer, John Farnham. As I watched him sing, he was passion personified. What energy and feeling! It was obvious he had committed himself to making the most of his gift. He had made singing a priority in his life and his gift was flourishing.

> *Whatever you make a priority will grow. You can tell your priorities by what time you spend, effort you make, thoughts you have, and the passion you execute on the things in your life.*

Like John's singing, whatever you make a priority will grow. You can tell your priorities by what time you spend, effort you make, thoughts you have, and the passion you execute, on the things in your life.

While what you pay attention to grows, likewise what you ignore dies. In working with people with addictions, I've discovered that the more someone thinks about a problem or an addiction, the more prone they are to grow it. We should be vigilant to pay no attention to the things in our lives that we would rather die than continue to grow.

We must learn to focus on what we can influence. All of us can influence family, friends, and even society. Generally that influence will come out of our strength. Most people try to focus on areas of their lives where they have very little strength or ability. The result is that they don't become an influence. Not only do they lack influence, they often fail and therefore lose focus.

Many will remember Michael Jordan's attempt to move into baseball. While Michael is a phenomenal basketball player, nobody wanted to 'be just like Mike' when it came to baseball. Why? It was the wrong focus.

When you focus, when all your energies come together at a focal point, great things will happen.

When you focus, when all your energies come together at a focal point, great things happen. Your focused efforts will bring productivity. Let me illustrate. Mother Theresa was a great humanitarian. But she didn't work with every single needy person. She focused on one core group of people in Calcutta. Out of that focal point, she became an influence on the planet. Mother Theresa could only be in one place at one time. Yet when she focused on something, she was able to influence many people in many places at any time. But the key was focus. Another example is Bill Gates III of Microsoft. He focused on software - not making computers - and his company has become a driving force in the new economy.

One dictionary defines focus as "The ability to define, to adjust one's eyes so that the image is clear". Focus helps you adjust your thinking and your strengths so something not only becomes clear but achievable in your life. You'll only succeed with the opportunities that you focus on. You're only able to hit the targets you truly aim at.

> *You'll only succeed with the opportunities that you focus on. You're only able to hit the targets you truly aim at.*

You can only be an influence in the area that you focus. Why is Tiger Woods so great at what he does? The answer is focus. Why are people successful in many fields of life and influential in those areas? Because they focus. Focus also gives you an advantage of becoming skilled and an expert at what you do.

The Extra Mile

The third element is *the principle of the extra mile*. Success, wealth and influence are never built on the average. They are always built on going the extra mile. If you only do what you've always done, you'll always get what you've always had. So if you want to make the most of an opportunity, you've got to go the extra mile, not just do what everybody else does.

Someone once commented that of all the faults in human beings the one we excuse most easily is idleness. Idleness won't bring about achievement. The extra mile will.

Procrastination Assassinates Opportunity

What are some enemies of the extra mile? Idleness and procrastination! Constantly putting something off rather than going the extra mile to achieve, will assassinate dreams, hopes, visions, wealth and even well being.

For example, if someone gave you the opportunity to join a gym, all expenses paid, with your own personal trainer, would you do as most people would – declare what a great opportunity it was and then put off starting until tomorrow? Would you go the extra mile – get up early, get yourself dressed, brave the cold and put in the hard yards? The opportunity is there, the trainer is there, and the gym is there. It's all there. The only thing stopping taking full advantage of the opportunity is procrastination. Idleness kills opportunity. Rather than sit back, go the extra mile and take the opportunity.

Laziness is another enemy of the extra mile. The lazy are always wanting to do something, when all they need to do is take the opportunities they have and go the extra mile with them. Laziness will always leave you wanting, but never doing. One thing is certain, if you overcome laziness and go the extra mile, you'll be on your way to making the most of your opportunity. The extra mile, my friends, is not a cluttered highway. At times it can be a very lonely road, but its rewards far outweigh those of the cluttered highways of indifference, idleness and procrastination.

There is a great story in our Australian history. Many of you may not be aware that the liberation of Beersheba in the Middle East came about by the bravery of 800 Light Horsemen. It was a victory that Napoleon could not achieve. Nor could the combined European armies of 11 different Crusades. Instead, the seemingly impossible happened when a group of young men literally went the extra mile.

Someone once said to me that the reason the Australians took Beersheba is that it is prefixed with the word 'beer'. Whilst I don't doubt that, I want you to read their story written by my friend Col Stringer.

Light Horsemen Liberate Jerusalem

The youngest nation on earth liberated the capital of one of the oldest nations on earth, Jerusalem, which had been under Muslim rule for almost 1600 years.

In the First World War 800 Australian Light Horsemen spearheaded the liberation of the Holy Land and God's chosen city – Jerusalem – from almost 1600 years of Muslim rule and domination.

In the Middle East, the Turks held the fortresses of Gaza-Beersheba. Any attacking army had to travel several days through the waterless Sinai desert under merciless sun, even to start an attack on Beersheba.

All the Turks had to do was hold off an attack for one day before the attackers would have run out of water and began to die in the desert heat, as had happened to many other armies throughout history.

Unlike cavalry of the Middle Ages, the Light Horsemen ride to the battle, dismount and fight the enemy on foot. And that is what the enemy expected.

The Light Horsemen lived by an unwritten code of ethics; you never left a 'mate' no matter what the cost! They were characterised by an ability to think and act for themselves under pressure. They sought out opportunity to beat the odds.

The Light Horsemen had to attempt what was unheard of in modern warfare, a cavalry charge across 6 kilometres of flat terrain straight into the machine guns and artillery canons of the 4500 enemy soldiers.

As the sun set, in the dying moments of October 31, 1917, the Light Horsemen seized the opportunity and charged!

The speed and tenacity of the charge took the enemy by surprise. The sights on artillery and guns couldn't be altered fast enough and shells and bullets whizzed over the heads of the charging Australians.

The Australian Light Horsemen achieved what 11 different ancient crusades, with the combined armies of five European nations, could not do. They achieved what the greatest military genius of his day, Napoleon, could not do, what 58,000 British troops could not do.

The first squadrons of Light Horsemen charged on over the enemy's trenches straight on to Beersheba. For the first time in 400 years they had opened the road to Jerusalem.

Eight hundred men spearheaded the defeat of an army and started the liberation of Jerusalem. They ended 1600 years of tyranny against Christians and Jews.

Later in Jerusalem a young ANZAC soldier climbed to the top of the Tower of David and unfurled a Jewish flag for the first time in centuries.

One of my favourite quotes from Winston Churchill is this one: "Continuous effort, not strength or intelligence, is the key to unlocking your potential." It's not the 'have-a-shot-at-one-thing-once' that gets you to success. Can you imagine if you approached marriage like that? You can't build a great marriage out of one conversation, one gift. It's a continual effort. It's a continual communication. Marriages need constant monitoring, maintaining, going the extra mile, persevering through the hardships. The strength of a marriage is formed in times of perseverance and stick-ability, not when everything's going well.

"Continuous effort, not strength or intelligence, is the key to unlocking your potential."
Winston Churchill

Consider the diamond. The diamond is ugly carbon made beautiful and priceless under pressure over time. Our character becomes equally priceless if we stick it out through the hard times. Napoleon Hill said, "Effort only fully releases its reward after a person refuses to quit."

CHAPTER FOUR

Never, Never, Say Die

Genius, a power that dazzles humans,
is oft but perseverance in disguise.

H.W. Austin

Humans tend to lose easily and win through effort and hard work. Most often when someone remarks, "I wish I had that opportunity", they really mean they missed the same opportunity. Missing out, however, doesn't mean the end. It can always become a new beginning.

In 1996, Greg Norman, the great Australian golfer, known affectionately as the 'Great White Shark', was on target to win the US Open. It was a feat that, despite a winning career, he had not yet achieved. Norman was well ahead of the other players. The media were certain of his pending victory, when inex-

plicably his game fell apart and the famous green jack-
et eluded him again. The next day the newspaper
headlines ran: "The Shark Can't Swim", "The Shark
Sinks", and "The Shark's Lost His Bite". At the end of
it all he said this: "I'm a winner. I lost today, but I'm
not a loser in life. I've won tournaments and I've lost
tournaments. Maybe something good is waiting to
happen. This is just a test."

Norman understood that the loss of one opportunity didn't mean the loss of all opportunity. Opportunity
abounds. So you lost an opportunity; well get ready
because there is anoth-
er one not far off.

Today, with the
changes in the way
people are doing busi-
ness, opportunity
abounds for everybody
to be successful. We
need to understand
that those who make
the most of opportuni-

*While successful
people go out after
their opportunity, most
others are waiting for
their chance to come
to them.*

ty, HAVE made the most of their opportunities, so it's
not too late to begin to find an opportunity now. They
haven't procrastinated on opportunities. While successful people go out after their opportunity, most others are waiting for their chance to come to them.

Opportunities, in fact, are never lost – the other guy
gets all the ones you miss! So if you don't want to continue to miss them, you've got to make some decisions.
Decide you will not miss your next opportunity.

Decide you will prepare for your next opportunity. Decide you will not give up.

Beverley Sills, the operatic soprano, beautifully summed up many people's fear of failure when she said, "You may be disappointed if you fail, but you're doomed if you don't try." Any person who chooses not to quit their dream is already on the verge of breaking into new levels of opportunity and success. I love this brilliant quote by renowned anthropologist William Strong, "The only time you don't fail is the last time you try anything and it works." Most people give up an opportunity without even trying it. They give in before they even give themselves a chance to make the most of an opportunity.

So what does it take to not be a quitter? A mind that is resolved! It is amazing what our minds can resolve to do and not do. Developing a mindset that will not give up helps us get over the past to score goals in life. Author and commentator George E. Woodbury said, "Defeat is not the worst of failures, not to have tried is true failure."

Here are three keys to help you resist the urge to quit.

Keep Trying

The first key is, *if you've failed, keep trying*. Before any great discovery in the field of medicine, or any healing of physical ailments, there is one common element – all have been preceded by failure. Scientists, doctors and healers all had failures before they had success. But the other thing they have in common is they did not give up. Ed Fredrick Douglas, US civil libertarian, put it this way: "Without a struggle there can be no progress." Often times, the greater the struggle, the greater and sweeter the victory.

What joy would there be if the journey to our achievements were just a luxury cruise? Absolutely none! Great joy comes out of struggle and achievement – that feel-

> *Before any great discovery in the field of medicine, or any healing of physical ailments, there is one common element - all have been preceded by failure.*

ing of self worth one gets after doing what others couldn't do or said was impossible. When they failed and quit, you didn't give up. Endurance is one of the greatest qualities in non-quitters. Develop the ability, like the rubber ball, to keep bouncing back. British social reformer, Thomas Buxton, said, "With ordinary talent and extraordinary perseverance all things are attainable."

My friend, Brian Houston, international speaker and pastor of Australia's largest church, says there are three ways people learn in life. The best way to learn is through other people's mistakes. The second-best way to learn is learn from your own mistakes. And the third way people learn? According to Brian, the worst way to learn – people don't learn from anyone's mistakes or their own mistakes. My friends, don't repeat the mistakes of other people; they missed their day of opportunity – don't miss yours! Learn from your own mistakes.

How many opportunities have you missed? Ask yourself – is there a possibility I can go back and take that opportunity? If there is, do it. Right now, someone probably has created an opportunity for you. Are you taking it, or are you missing it? Don't repeat the same mistakes – missing opportunities and letting them go by. Learn from those mistakes. It is a tragedy that some people don't take heed of their own or anyone else's mistakes. Learn from history not to miss an opportunity. Learn from your own experience not to give up. Take the opportunities you are given.

> *"The majority of men meet with failure because of their lack of persistence in creating new plans [opportunities] to take the place of those which fail."*
> *Napoleon Hill*

A quote from Napoleon Hill sums it up: "The majority of men meet with failure because of their lack of persistence in creating new plans [opportunities] to take the place of those which fail." What opportunities, what new plans, what new ways of doing things, new sources of income, new strategies and plans are in place now that weren't around ten or 20 years ago? These plans have been created for you to take over past plans which have failed. These opportunities will create even more opportunities for your future. The key is to take your opportunities now.

Will opportunities involve risk? Yes! Will these opportunities always be there? Maybe not. Is there a chance of failure? Yes! Is there a chance to succeed? Absolutely! The key is to take them.

Never Lower Your Aim

The next key to redeeming lost opportunities is to *never lower your aim*. Where do you want to be? What does your future look like? What is your dream? Now consider how you will get there. What mechanism, what plan, strategy or business do you currently have that's going to take you there? If you don't have one, you must find one. You are only going to be successful in achieving your aim if you've got the right mechanism, the right vehicle to get you there.

Most people want to achieve wealth. I don't know anyone who doesn't want or need more money. But when it comes to earning more, most people do the 'same-old', 'same-old', hoping they'll hit the jackpot, win the lottery, or somehow get the million dollar TV quiz prize. That, my friends, is living in fantasy. They've got a high aim but they've got no method to get there. You've got to aim high and work strategically towards achieving it. Start positioning yourself in a situation that will create wealth for you. Learn to derive income that will help you build a strong asset

> *"If you want to be successful, find someone you can model yourself on."*

base from which you can further increase your income. Seek out advice from people who achieve where and what you want to achieve.

The best motivational speakers and business leaders in the world will always tell you, "If you want to be successful, find someone you can model yourself on." In my life, I've got fantastic role models whom I want to follow. I think of heroes like Billy Graham, Nelson Mandela and Martin Luther King Jr. They all aimed high and achieved the impossible. They all had someone else they looked up to. They all created a vehicle to get to where they wanted to go ... and so must you.

You've got to aim high, higher than yourself. If all we aim at is average, all we will ever get is average. Generally, with what you aim at, you'll either come just a little under or over. So aim high, plan strategically, and act decisively. We need to train hard so that we can win easily.

> *It's what you do with the time you've got that determines the life you live.*

One of our great Australian Olympians is a young lady by the name of Melinda Gainsford-Taylor. Melinda is known to practise her running by trailing a car tyre behind her. Now let me ask you this question: will she ever have to enter an Olympic Games with a tyre attached to her body? The answer is no, but it means she builds strength in her running so that when she actually does run a race, she can win more easily.

Friends, it's imperative to learn that we must train hard to achieve things. Training hard makes winning look simple. Any top athlete, swimmer, football player, or basketball player will train more than they actually play. Each week they invest hour upon hour of weight training, sprints, ball handling, stroke training. Why? Because if they train hard, they can win easily, and they won't quit before they win!

A few years ago, my favourite football team in Australia was given little if any chance of getting into the season's semi-finals. At the beginning of the year, they hated their endurance-training coach. He made them do the extra sprints, when other teams were just relaxing a little. In the off season, he made them run along beaches. He made them sprint-train. He forced them to do extra weights. They hated Billy Johnson. But at the end of the year at the final play-offs, when some of the games had to go into extra time and they won, not only well, but convincingly, when they finished the match with greater strength than many of their weary and tired opponents, they loved coach Billy. They actually celebrated him, almost more than their victories. They over trained so they could over perform. They trained hard to win easily. They didn't cut corners, they didn't take short cuts, and they didn't quit. When others were relaxing, they

Perserverance is not one long race, it's one short race after another.

worked hard. And eventually it brought them incredible victory and the respect of even the most vehement opposition. Remember: train hard, don't quit!

Perseverance is not one long race, it's one short race after another.

Make up Lost Time

The next key is to *make up lost time*. One of my observations of life in general is this: most people get ahead during the times that others waste. Think how many people today are the fastest remote control changer on the planet, yet cannot find a way out of their financial situations. All of us get 24 hours in a day, yet some people achieve so much more than others do. Some people can make more in one hour than most people make in a month of work. People might say, "That's not fair!" But it most definitely is fair. It is fair because there are those who waste time and others who make the most of time.

> *Time is a gift we all get so we need to use it wisely.*

Time is a gift we all get so we need to use it wisely, effectively, efficiently and opportunistically. It's what you do with the time you've got that determines the life you live. What you do with the opportunities you are given, at the time they are given to you, determines your success or failure.

As a speaker, I have noticed that some people given 60 minutes on a subject leave you wondering what on earth they just said. Others get 10 minutes and you are left thinking what an incredible message, having sat on the edge of your seat gasping for more. I believe the difference is the amount of time people put into their preparation for speaking. It's the same in life. The amount of time you've spent in working your opportunity, building your opportunity, researching, and planning your opportunity will determine whether it's a success or a failure. That choice is yours ...

CHAPTER FIVE

Decide to Decide
to Be Decisive

Decision is a sharp knife that cuts clean and straight.
Indecision is a dull one that hacks and tears
and leaves ragged edges behind it.

Gordon Graham

Some time ago, award-winning vocal artist, Gloria Estefan, made a brilliant statement in one of her songs: "We seal our fate by the choices we make." Choices determine destinies. Wishes don't determine our destiny in life. Wants never fulfil our dreams. Choices determine destiny and dreams.

Every day we make choices. At times we don't even realize we are making them. Getting out of bed each morning is a choice. For some people it's a major miracle! But for most of us it is a choice we don't even consider we've made. Going to work is a choice; getting married is a choice. Choices are an every day part of life, but very few people pay attention to the choices they make. In fact, I would say that most people pay little or no attention to the choices they make and therefore don't live the kind of lives they really want to. Instead they live the life that fate or lack of decision-making makes for them. Rather than actively choosing what kind of life they want to live, they let life just happen to them. What you choose ultimately determines your behaviour, your financial situation and your friends.

To pursue opportunities in our lives and to maximise their potential, we must be people of decision. History is full of people having come face-to-face with opportunity. Many have made great decisions. Some, however, have made poor decisions and borne the consequences. Manuscripts of the movie and book *Gone with the Wind* were initially rejected. They were choices, and bad ones at that! The *Titanic* is another famous example of a series of ridiculous and disastrous choices for which many paid the ultimate price.

We are all accountable for our behaviour. By choosing our behaviour, we choose the consequences and circumstances of our lives. Accepting this law stops us from dodging, ducking and weaving around questions about why our life is the way it is. You may say, "Hey – hang on a minute, Pat. I've been hurt. I've had divorce happen to me. I've had business failures. I've had … "

That may be the case, but are you responsible for those hurts? NO. Are you accountable for your response to them? YES.

No matter what has happened to us, no matter what our circumstances, we must accept that our behavioural decisions will determine the outcome of our lives. Whether we choose to believe it or not, we own our feelings – they are ours, no one else's. To choose to feel the way we do, to live in the situation we do, is our choice and ours alone. We need to learn to *choose* 'better' so we can *live* 'better' and *have* 'better'.

> **We need to learn to choose 'better' so we can live 'better' and have 'better'.**

If I don't like my job, I need to make the right decision. If I am unhappy with my weight, I need to make the right decision. If I don't trust people, I need to make the decision to begin to trust. If I am not happy, I can choose to change.

Blame

Many people throw the blame for their problems onto something else, whether it is their spouse, a workmate or a lack of opportunity. When we blame others we abdicate the responsibility to change. What they are actually doing is not defining the real problem. A problem well defined is a problem solved. If we don't diagnose correctly, we are not going to treat the problem correctly, and things won't get better.

Ask yourself: What is in my life that I don't like?

What can I do to change the situation? Ask yourself: What did I do to get into this situation? Did I not trust? Did I fail to be clear about what I wanted? Did I fail to set goals? Did I choose to befriend the wrong person at the wrong time? Did I choose the wrong time? Did I miss the opportunity? Did I fail to stand up for what I believe is right? Did I fail to ask for what I wanted? Did I not ask enough? Did I not get up and do what I meant to? Did I procrastinate? We must face responsibility for the choices that will determine our opportunities.

Stop the Blame Game

There is an oft quoted saying, "You shall know the truth and the truth shall set you free". Facing up to truth is a choice. It is at the very core of human nature to blame others. Blame is a type of self-preservation, an escape mechanism for us. We don't want things to be our responsibility, so we rationalise our actions and go to any extreme to blame others. But such action doesn't solve any-thing. It's your life, it's your financial situation, it's your feelings – there-fore, you must make the decisions that will affect you and your future. Peter Drucker, one of the 20th century's most progressive business thinkers, says it this way, "Once the facts are clear the decisions jump out at you."

"Once the facts are clear the decisions jump out at you"
Peter Drucker

I remember a time when I lost my car keys. Every

husband knows that when you've lost the car keys, your wife has them! Well, my wife and I looked everywhere. We searched all over the house; in the drawers, in our cupboards, between the seats on the lounge, but we didn't find the keys. Why? Because they weren't in the house! I had left those keys in the ignition of my car! When we try to blame others, it's exactly the same situation. I was looking to point blame that simply wasn't there.

You make the choices, you say the words, you settle too easily, you quit, you talk yourself down, you sell out your dreams, you choose your job, you let people treat you the way they do, you feel rejected, you trust the untrustworthy. You choose how you feel, how you react and how you deal with the unexpected. US editor, novelist and essayist, E.W. Howe stated, "People storm imaginary Alps and die in the foothills cursing difficulties that do not exist." When we appoint blame we are expending the energy we could be applying to defining and overcoming the real problem.

> *"People storm imaginary Alps and die in the foothills cursing difficulties that do not exist."*
> E. W. Howe

We are more responsible for our decisions than we think. People want a successful future, yet every night they sit in front of the television and 'veg-out', instead of getting up and building that future. They want a better marriage, so what do they do? They sit watching old re-runs of TV soap operas rather than spending time with family and children. It doesn't take long before this becomes a pattern of behaviour. Unfortunately, some of our behaviour becomes automatic. We stop paying attention to it and no longer evaluate its emotional and financial effect on our lives.

Problems won't go away, financial situations won't go away, and they don't get better with time unless we make a decision to change something. What we don't admit is wrong or is not where it ought to be will only get worse until we do. To admit things are wrong with your life is to take the opportunity to make decisions that will change the course of your life.

The famous explorer David Livingstone once said, "I am prepared to go anywhere provided it be forward." If you want to seize the opportunities that come your way then you must make that same decision – to move forward. You must decide to create the future you want. Those who do not create the future they want must endure the future they get.

Do What Others Won't Do

I believe the difference between winners and losers in life is that winners take action and make the decisions that losers don't want to take and make. Like an athlete we need to review our life's performance in light of results. When we do this, we don't accept excuses. There is no reason not to reach our goal.

Nothing in our life will change unless we begin to do something different. If you want to get something you've never had, you've got to do something you've never done. Former US Secretary of State, John Foster Dulles said, "The measure of success is not whether you have a tough problem to deal with, but whether it is the same problem you had last year".

If you are struggling with the same problems, obstacles, financial struggles and habits as those you faced ten years, five years, even a year ago, then you have not made the choice to break out from them and get on with life's opportunities.

> "The measure of success is not whether you have a tough problem to deal with, but whether it is the same problem you had last year."
> John Foster Dulles

It's a mistake to assume that life will get better when no decision has been made towards that betterment. I believe the best way to predict influence and live in the future we want, is to make a decision to create it. Gandhi put it this way, "We must become the change we seek in the world and that takes a decision."

We commonly think that people's lives are better because they have had the luck of the draw. Or they've been brought up in a wealthy environment with a silver spoon in their mouth. You can be brought up with a silver spoon or, as in my case, brought up with a wooden spoon! It's irrelevant. What matters are the choices you make to take hold of opportunities that come your way! When you grasp those opportunities, they become a powerful mechanism to springboard you into your future, and to create a future for others.

Just recently I was reading an article which described what in many cases happened to the fortunes millionaires left to their children. All too often this hard-won wealth was squandered and wasted. Those children had an opportunity to better themselves, to create more wealth from the finances they inherited. But because of bad decisions, they actually lost the resource that was given to them. What an opportunity! Yet their decisions caused them to lose the goldmine they inherited.

Be Like Mike: Make A Decision

An environment of opportunity surrounds our lives – it's everywhere. Some people make a decision to act on it, while others make a decision to leave it. A great example is one of the 20th century's greatest sporting heroes – Michael Jordan. When Michael Jordan soars through the air to slam-dunk a basketball, it seems like time stands still. Many people have referred to his ability as 'Magic'. Kids want to be just like Mike. At the peak of his career Michael had many opportunities before him – multi-million dollar contracts and advertising agencies wanting to secure his endorsements.

> *An environment of opportunity surrounds our lives - it's everywhere. Some people make a decision to act on it, while others make a decision to leave it.*

But Michael's life wasn't always filled with opportunity. In fact, he was dropped from his high school basketball team.

Gloria Estefan can move a crowd. Together with her band she can have an audience standing on their feet singing, clapping and dancing, simply by singing a few notes.

It can all seem as if these people just had success thrust upon them. Or that they just got a lucky break. Maybe they were just at the right place at the right time. You can have all these factors. You can be at the right place at the right time. You can get a great break. You can receive an open door of opportunity. But here's what separates the Gloria Estefans, the Michael Jordans and the other successful people of our world – they make a decision to act on the opportunities they are given; and choose not to live in their past failures or fears. They decide to live their childhood dreams.

Faced with adversity they chose not to quit on their dreams. As I have told you, Michael Jordan was cut from his high school basketball team and had to become the team manager in order to keep practising with the rest of the players. He said of those days, "If there was a most likely to succeed, I was the least."

It is always too early to give up on your dreams.

Gloria Estefan had her back broken in a traffic accident at the height of her career and underwent intensive physical therapy to return to the stage.

It is always too early to give up on your dreams.

Imagine if Neil Armstrong had given up on his childhood dream to do something great in aviation. He would never have been the first human being to step onto the surface of the moon.

Opportunity lies inside us from our earliest days. As a young girl Barbra Streisand could think of little else than becoming a professional entertainer. Andrew Lloyd Webber, famous for the stage productions *Phantom of the Opera* and *Evita*, spent hours as a child constructing elaborate sets for the puppet shows with which he entertained the family.

It's always too early to decide to quit on your opportunities!

Let me give you a personal example. I write books and speak all over the world because it feeds my greater dream of helping others. For the same reason, I became the Executive Director of a drug rehabilitation centre. The centre houses many young men from all around my home state. Every day, my 'boys' as I call them have to make decisions in life that you and I will probably never have to make. They have to make a decision not to go back to a life of crime and drug addiction. They have to make a decision to stay in long-term rehabilitation. They have to decide to persevere when they read books, study and do personal development, even though some of them don't have the most academic minds or have the best literary ability. It's a tough decision, but they make that decision.

I've seen these young men develop into outstanding citizens because they make the decision to take a window of opportunity that's been given to them.

Someone has given them an opportunity to get their life together. Someone has given them an opportunity to break their addictions and enter into a life of success. Someone has given them an opportunity to take control of their life and develop the skills needed to build a future and have a family, rather than live a life of crime.

Those who don't stick it out, quitting in the midst of their opportunity, generally go back to the same lifestyle.

Some of these young men make the decision and stick with it. Having made it, they rarely return to their former life. In fact, the centre has an 86-percent success rate for those who stick with the program to its completion. They never return to the past. Those who don't stick it out, quitting in the midst of their opportunity, generally go back to the same lifestyle. It's all in the ability to choose.

CHAPTER SIX

Don't Fear It, Face It

*The men who try to do something and fail
are infinitely better than those who
try to do nothing and succeed.*

Dr Martyn Lloyd-Jones

Overcoming Hindrances to Opportunity

Franklin D. Roosevelt was President of the USA even though he had been crippled by polio. Artist, Henri Matisse, created some of his greatest work when aged, bed-ridden and nearly blind. Patty Catalano, one of history's top women marathon runners, overcame the self-destructive habits of overeating and chain smoking to become a world class athlete. Thomas Edison's father called him a dunce, and his headmaster told him he would never make a success of anything.

Henry Ford barely made it through high school.

The father of the Polaroid camera, Edwin Land, after failing to develop instant movies, turned his efforts to easy photography. He described the challenge before him in this way: "... trying to use an impossible chemistry in a non-existent technology to make an un-manufacturable product for which there was no discernible demand." That, in his opinion, created the optimum working conditions for a creative mind. While most of us have used his invention, the result of his perseverance, too many of us still live under the power of obstacles rather than the limitlessness of opportunity.

What are some of the obstacles that people are afraid of? Take a moment to look at the list below, consider your fears, and reflect on the company you keep.

(Tick the ones that apply to you)

I lack education!	Henry Ford
I don't know enough people!	Al Gore
I have a family history of failure!	Abraham Lincoln
I have a physical disability!	Helen Keller
I was abused as a child!	Oprah Winfrey
I have a criminal history!	Nelson Mandela
Nobody understands my dream!	Walt Disney
I'm too old!	Cher (just kidding!) At 82, Winston Churchill wrote his history of the English people.
I'm too young!	Nadia Comenici, aged 14, achieved

I have an illness!

The timing's not right yet!

I've been rejected in the past!

I'm not good at
communicating with people!

gymnastics' perfect
score of 10 at the
Montreal Olympics
in 1976.
Champion US
cyclist Lance
Armstrong.
In 1856, Italian
Antonio Meucci
set up the world's
first phone line, but
he never marketed
his idea. A few
years later German
Johann Philipp
Reis made a device
he dubbed a tele
phone. Almost 20
years later,
Alexander Graeme
Bell created the
modern phone,
filed his patent
papers, and reaped
the glory.
Colonel Sanders,
Abraham Lincoln
… and just about
anyone else who's
achieved anything!

Moses

Think about this ... all of these fears and excuses, whether imagined or real, are used by people to forsake or dismiss opportunity. Yet, it's those very things that can catapult you into success.

Face Your Fears

Fear is a terrible thing. My good friend, Robert Ferguson, a leading pastor and teacher, recently gave some advice on fear. Two of the most important points he made were that fear is a tool used to cripple our destiny, and fear is real to the person who is experiencing it. For example, I am not at all afraid of cockroaches, but my wife and daughters are terrified of them. Women amaze me – they can pour hot wax on themselves, and rip hair like you wouldn't believe, but be terrified by a tiny cockroach! My attitude is, "You're so big, it's so little – so deal with it!" What terrifies them means nothing to me. But their fear of cockroaches is very real to them!

We can all face our fears by changing our view of the things that concern us. We need a new pair of binoculars. Robert Ferguson suggests that when you have a set of binoculars and you look at them through the small holes, everything is magnified. We need to look at our fears through the big lens. That way

> *When you have a set of binoculars and you look at them through the small holes, everything is magnified. We need to look at our fears through the big lens.*

everything else gets small and you get big. How you view yourself is how you view your fear and how others view you. Change your perceptions so that you can face your fears.

Reject Rejection

What are those fears? Most people are afraid of rejection. They fear it more than they do missing their opportunity. They fear that an opportunity may cause them to lose friends, prestige, and associations. Isn't it strange how success can bring you great friends but can also cause you to feel rejected? I remember when I was a kid, we would play in the school grounds and always pick the biggest macho guys to play on our team. You remember those guys – the type who had muscles on their fingernails! We would line up, and I'd look at the team leaders and silently wish, "Pick me, pick me!" Finally, there were just two people left, the nerd and I – and they would pick him first! Talk about rejection!

Rejection starts when we are kids, and we bring it into our adult life. We all crave acceptance. Unfortunately, most people would rather be liked than respected. People like other people to be average. People like those who don't rise to the top. But we remember people

> *Unfortunately, most people would rather be liked than respected.*

whose values we aspire to: courage, conviction, character, initiative and willingness to make a go of an opportunity. Fear of rejection, by contrast, causes people to accept lives of conformity and mediocrity. Fear of rejection causes people to crave acceptance and popularity. But you can't satisfy something that comes from inside you, with external factors like popularity polls or other people's opinions. We must decide to live by purpose, not fickle popularity.

The fear of rejection causes people to by-pass opportunity because they don't really understand who they are. There is a story told of some men who had been prisoners of war in a Nazi concentration camp.

> *Fear of rejection causes people to by-pass opportunity.*

At the end of the war these poor specimens of inhumane suffering had lost their memories. They could not remember their names, or to whom they belonged. So it was decided to have these men tour from hall to hall around Europe. Their photographs were posted up and if anyone recognized them, they were to come to collect them at the various viewing halls.

On one such day, the hall was packed. People came to collect their sons, fathers, and uncles, barely recognizable because of the injustice they had suffered. However, no-one came for a particular man, so he stood out in front of the crowd and asked, "Does anybody know who I am? Can anybody tell me to whom I belong?" That man said what most people think and feel. We all desire to belong, and there is nothing wrong with that. But when the craving to belong overcomes your desire to fulfil a dream and opportunity, when the fear of rejection is greater than the power of opportunity, you've got a problem. The tragic equation goes like this:

Self worth = Performance + Other people's opinions

Instead, we need to overcome the fear of rejection and grab hold of opportunities by adopting this formula:

Self worth = Resolve your identity + Choose to stand for something + Unfurl your dreams + Create a new reality

Let's look at some of these ingredients in the formula for self worth.

Resolve Your Identity
Many of us have asked the question, "Who am I?" (Notice I didn't ask what you do - that's your *function*, not who you are.) Let's look at some of the things you are or can be:

I am successful	I can be successful
I am an achiever	I can be an achiever
I am a leader	I can be a leader
I am a dreamer	I can be a dreamer

You've just defined your identity. If you resolve that this is who you are, you won't need continual affirmation from people, and you won't let your feelings dictate whether you bail out of an opportunity or not.

Arnold Schwarzenegger is a great example of such resolute self-affirmation. He says this:

The mind is the limit. As long as the mind can envisage the fact that you can do something, you really can do it – as long as you really believe it 100%. It's all mind over matter. All I know is that the first step is to create the vision, because when you see the vision there – the beautiful vision – that creates the "want power". For example, my wanting to be Mr Universe came about because I saw myself so clearly, being up there on the stage and winning.

Choose to Stand for Something

Choose to stand for something, not blend with everything. I find it amazing that people want to be different, yet they are all the same. They do business the same, they build the same houses, and their beliefs are the same. They have never taken the opportunity to be different, to do things differently.

I remember some years ago going to a school where there were 1200 students in the audience. At the front was a group of girls all dressed like Madonna. (Do you remember when Madonna had her hair like Marge Simpson?) This group of girls were all dressed the same. Their hairstyles were the same, their make-up was (you guessed it) the same. I asked them, "Why are you girls all dressed like Madonna?" The ringleader replied, "Because we want to be different." And yet they were all the same! It's time that we allowed ourselves to be different and shun conformity. Our world suffers from conformity in this age of political correctness. We are afraid to define things as they should be, or ever say things as we feel. We're even afraid to live in the opportunities we are presented with because of our politically correct thinking. Consider for a moment the words we use to define certain things:

If you are Short, you are Vertically Challenged.

Gingerbread Men are now called Gingerbread People.

If you have a Bad Temper, you are Anger Enhanced.

If you are a Drug Addict, you are called Chemically Inconvenienced.

If you are Lazy, you are Motivationally Dispossessed.

But my favourite is this:

If you are a Thief or Shoplifter (wait for it), you are now called a Non-Traditional Shopper.

Can you imagine going to court and being charged for non-traditional shopping to support your chemical inconvenience, because you were motivationally dispossessed to the degree you could do nothing with your life? Yet people live this way, because of the fear of rejection, and miss out on opportunities.

Herbert Bayard Swope, NY *World* editor and politician, said it best: "I cannot give you the formula for success, but I can give you the formula for failure which is 'try to please everybody'."

Unfurl Your Dreams

We hide our dreams. We love them but are embarrassed by them. Maybe we feel we are not worthy of the dream. That old fear – "Who do you think you are?" – cripples us. In life, if you're constantly told you can't, you probably never will. We program ourselves into thinking we can't by constantly telling ourselves we can't. So when opportunities come to us that can give us a new perspective, put us on a road to financial freedom or be a highway for our dreams, we don't grab that opportunity because we've talked ourselves into believing we can't handle it, before we even begin.

Create a New Reality

Our lives will never be the same. It's an exciting time for all. The key is to enter the 21st century with a brand new view of a how things can get done.

I am reminded of the movie *Truman*. It is the story of a young man living in a world created for him by the egotistical media mogul, Christos. Truman lives in a fake world of actors, each playing their part. His wife, family and friends are all actors. It is a world he is born into and does not know any better. In essence he is trapped. Sound familiar? Of course it does: that's the story of most people – trapped in a world and work environment someone else planned. Trapped in a job where someone else calls the shots, moves the players in motion at his or her will without regard for your dreams, desires and ambition.

Truman, however, discovers he is trapped and plans his escape. He faces opposition on every side, even from his family and friends. They use fear, threats and distractions to keep him from escaping. Finally, it almost costs him his life, but Truman's will and desire to be free are stronger than the pain of the challenge. He walks through the door to a new reality, a free man! The question is, will you?

We can all achieve our dreams if we choose to take the opportunities given to us.

Don't allow yourself to feel trapped any longer. You can walk through the door of opportunity. All of us can learn to become free. We can all achieve our dreams if we choose to take the opportunities given to us. Those opportunities may come to us packaged as adversity, but we can all learn to see beyond the struggle and capture greater success.

What exciting concept or opportunity are you looking at right now? What great opportunity is available to you? What can you start to do about personal happiness and financial freedom? Maybe you know of a way to build a business enabling you to establish a world-wide financial base for the 21st century, but are afraid to get in! Don't be. Your opportunity day is today!

CHAPTER SEVEN

Giving

*There is no more noble occupation in the world,
than to assist another human being and
to help some one succeed.*

Alan Loy McGinnis

Creating Opportunity for Others

One of the greatest laws in the universe is the law of
sowing and reaping. Put another way, what you sow in
life, you also reap.

We see this sowing principle in action all around us.
People who live generous, giving lives often receive
great rewards. Great friends attract equally great
friendships. And those who are lazy, more often than
not, live a life that's wasteful and unfulfilled. Since the
beginning of creation farmers have cultivated crops by

this same principle. They would never expect a crop which they hadn't planted in the first place. It is the same in our lives. Robert Kiyosaki in his brilliant book *Rich Dad, Poor Dad* states that whatever you want in life, you've got to give away first.

Isn't it amazing that the things you give away often return to you? I'll never forget one Sunday morning being invited to speak for a great friend of mine, Steve. It was his birthday and the crowd had brought a cake but no gift. That morning I had my favourite watch on. It was my pride and joy. Now

> *"Whatever you want in life, you've got to give away first."*
> Robert Kiyosaki

I have come to trust the prompts I get in my heart and that morning, as I spoke, I felt I should give my watch to Steve. I have got to tell you it was not an easy task. I had saved, I had planned, I had bargained for this watch. It was my dream watch, maybe not to anyone else's eyes or heart, but certainly to mine. All of a sudden I knew I had to give it away. Right there in the middle of my talk, I yelled to Steve, "Catch!" and threw him the watch. Fortunately he's a better catcher than I am a pitcher! Now Steve is a lot taller than I am, and he has the wrists to go with his height, but he was so overwhelmed by receiving this gift, he immediately put it on. His arm turned red, but I couldn't convince him to take it off until I gave him the extra links with it. Later Steve told me, "I always dreamed of having this watch." He said, "Pat, I'd watch you speak and I'd think I'd love a watch like that one."

So I followed my heart and gave that watch away. Can I tell you, from that day to this, I have had more watches given to me than I could ever need? I've been given a solid gold Rolex with a diamond bezel face. I've been given a beautiful Rolex Submariner. Let me tell you, when you give something away you will always get something better in return! Never miss the opportunity to give. Never disregard those heart-felt prompts, because what may seem silly to you might mean everything to someone else.

Seeds Turn into Harvests

I heard a man once say that one can count the seeds in an apple, but cannot count the apples in a seed. What seeds of opportunity are you creating for other people?

Opportunities don't just happen; they are created. We create opportunities when we share them, when we show them and when we give them away. We often think entrepreneurs are only creating wealth for themselves, when in fact they are also creating many opportunities for others. A successful venture creates job opportunities, wealth opportunities and opportunities for people to buy homes, not to mention opportunities for them to educate their children and create a future. Successful businesses help others fulfil their dreams.

Successful businesses help others fulfil their dreams.

Too often people denigrate the entrepreneurial spirit, a spirit and an attitude we so desperately need. Entrepreneurs are accused of opportunism. Let me say this – the person making the opportunities actually creates opportunities. We must learn to elevate those who create opportunities, not denigrate them. Anybody successful has sown seeds causing them to reap a harvest of prosperity. Former Chrysler Corporation chairman, Lee Iacocca, said, "In the end all business operations can be reduced to three words - people, product and profits. People come first."

> *"In the end all business operations can be reduced to three words – people, product and profits. People come first."*
> *Lee Iacocca*

A key to making the most of opportunity is to know that we must also create opportunities for others. Brian Tracy, author of *Maximum Achievement*, said, "Successful people are always looking for opportunities to help others, unsuccessful people are always asking what's in it for me?"

Creating Opportunity

We create opportunities by networking with other people. Networking is people working together for self-betterment. I enjoy being connected. I have lost count of the times I have been able to connect other people. Perhaps it was a printer who needed a great graphic artist, or a great graphic artist who needed someone to print something. Perhaps it was someone who was looking for an opportunity to become successful, and I had the opportunity to link him with someone who has been financially successful. Many times I have been able to help young people struggling with addictions and crisis in their life meet someone who has overcome similar difficulties. Their triumph has provided inspiration for those young people. This is connecting people together. It is the art of networking.

No man or woman will ever be a success by his or her self. We must learn the art of working together. It's the power of synergy, where the total sum is greater than the individual parts. Let me illustrate. A steering wheel is useless to us outside its functioning in a car. But without the steering wheel, every other component of the car is worthless. Taken together, the steering wheel, the engine, the transmission and every other individual part that makes up the car is very useful. Synergy is the power of each individual part working together.

> *No man or woman will ever be a success by him or her self. We must learn the art of working together.*

We can do collectively, with co-operation and with an interconnection, much more than we ever could just on our own. We see it in football, basketball and relay races. We see it in armies, clever organisations and successful marriages, where people work together for the betterment of everyone. It's called teamwork. The best organisations learn how to work together using each other's strengths to compensate each other's weaknesses. It's an age-old principle that has become even more powerful in this new millennium.

And that's how creating opportunities works. We create opportunities for others; they create opportunities for us. We are a stronger force together. I have many friends who are brilliant speakers, and often we will share information so that we can create opportunities for each other. I will refer their names to business organisations and convention planners and they do the same for me. It's the power of creating opportunities for other people.

Be ready for the opportunity that's created for you. Someone once said, "Be ready when opportunity comes. Luck is the time when preparation and opportunity meet." Former British Prime Minister, Benjamin Disraeli put it this way, "The secret of success in life is for a man to be ready for his opportunity when it comes." Are you ready for today's opportunities? Are you ready to create opportunities for others? All of your time, preparation and dreams come together in an opportunity that can become the vehicle through which you can build your future. Are you looking at an opportunity that has been created for you?

Created opportunities must be viewed as an act of generosity. The Roman

> "Be ready when opportunity comes. Luck is the time when preparation and opportunity meet."

author Seneca once said, "Wherever there is a human being, there is an opportunity for kindness." Mother Theresa said these words, "Unless life is lived for others, it's not worthwhile." As a young nun she developed a burning desire to work with the homeless and hopeless. Although she was convinced of this calling, her superiors suggested her youth and inexperience would cause her to fail in such an endeavour. At the age of 39 she was finally allowed to pursue her passion. Not only has she created opportunities for the poor and the needy, she has created opportunities for others to do the same. Through the work she started, many have found a sense of dignity and achievement in helping the less fortunate. Alan Loy McGinnis, author of *Friendship Factor*, said, "There is no more noble occupation in the world, than to assist another human being and to help someone succeed."

> "Wherever there is a human being, there is an opportunity for kindness."
> Seneca

Let me give you a timely illustration. In my books I often quote other writers and their great sayings of what others have done. They have created an opportunity for you and I to think. They have also created an opportunity for us to build on those precious few words they have given to us. They have created opportunity, and we in turn give them credit for their impartation to us.

To create an opportunity, you sometimes need to

give someone just a little push. A bird has incredible potential; it can fly! But as a chick it feels secure in its nest. It has to learn to fly in order to fulfil its potential, so a little push from its parent is needed. Soon the comfort of the nest is forgotten for the glory of soaring the high places. Sometimes, all someone needs is a bit of a push to believe they can achieve what they want to.

Be Sweet

Persuasion comes from the Latin word 'persuasio' which means, 'through sweetness'. We create opportunities for people, not by force, but through sweetness, showing them they can do it. That 'sweetness' comes in seeing things through their eyes. Most of us want to put people in their place. Our natural reaction is to expect people to do what we do. If we want to create opportunities for others, we must put ourselves in their place. We must look at life through their eyes.

In life, what you see is determined by where you stand. Where you stand determines what you see. If you want to persuade people and create opportunities for them you must put yourself in their circumstances and see what they see. This will help us in creating opportunities, but it will also help us become more persuasive in convincing them that the opportunities we create are worthwhile pursuing.

Once you create an opportunity for someone, and they become successful at it, don't be threatened by him or her. And vice versa, when someone creates an opportunity for you, be thankful for it! Decide to be a role model of opportunity-creation.

All of us can become teachers and heroes to some-body else. Children teach us this. If a boy believes in his parent enough, the parent can convince him of anything. I remember my daughter Chantelle beaming at me as I explained to her, when she was just a few years of age, that Daddy visited the moon on that day. And with big eyes, she said, "Really?" I had to explain to her that it wasn't actually true. It took more con-vincing to un-explain myself than it did to explain. In *The Natural*, Bernard Malamud states, "Without heroes, we are all plain people and don't know how far we can go." People generally don't improve unless they have someone else to model their lives upon. They have the attitude that, "If they can do it, I can do it!"

Author Charles Fowler put it this way, "The best teachers of humanity are the lives of great men." The most important influ-ence in another person's life isn't necessarily an event, although events influence us. It doesn't necessarily have to be a book or a story, either.

> *"Without heroes, we are all plain people and don't know how far we can go."*
> Bernard Malamud

The greatest influence can, and most often is, another person's life. You can decide to be that life – you will create opportunities for others, so they can follow in your footsteps.

When you create a network, opportunities tend to breed. With one opportunity comes another opportu-nity and then another. John Steinbeck, author of *The*

Grapes of Wrath, in a rather humorous way said, "Ideas are like rabbits. You get a couple and learn how to handle them and pretty soon you have a dozen." The same can be said of opportunities. I can create an opportunity for another person by introducing them to a friend. I can create opportunities by referring people to other people. I can create opportunities for people by giving them ideas. I can do it by introducing them to a business. I can create opportunities by being a role model to them, to help kick start their opportunity. I can create opportunities for others by taking an opportunity myself and inviting others to be part of it.

> *"Ideas are like rabbits. You get a couple and learn how to handle them and pretty soon you have a dozen."*
> *John Steinbeck*

There's a story about the entertainer Jimmy Durante and his performance in front of an audience of World War II veterans. Because of his busy schedule, he had originally agreed to a brief appearance. He delivered his short monologue, but lingered on the stage as the applause grew louder and louder. After half an hour, he took a bow. Backstage, he was asked why he had stayed so long. Jimmy pointed to the front row, where two one-armed veterans sat clapping enthusiastically. One had lost his right arm and the other his left, but they both used what they had together, and applauded him. His heart had gone out to these two men who, despite their limitations, in spite of what others might have seen as a handicap, had learned how to work together. They did the best they could with what they had. You can live a generous life helping others fulfil their dreams and all you need to do is start now …

CHAPTER EIGHT

Change

If you thought it yesterday,
if you're thinking it today,
you won't think it tomorrow.

Faith Popcorn

Every opportunity requires change. Change is that ugly word that people do their best to avoid. I remember someone once saying to me, "Pat, I'm like the Almighty: I changeth not." My response was, "He's perfect – you're not."

President John F. Kennedy said, "Change is the law of life. Those who only look to the past or present are certain to miss the future."

The future, my friends, is all about change. And change is about progress. We must change; our economies must change; business methods must change. Products change; distribution mechanisms change; leadership roles change; the way we lead changes. Our tastes are in a constant state of change. Even our body changes almost every single day without us even knowing. All this change requires effort. Civil-rights activist, the Rev. Jesse Jackson, said of change, "Tears will get you sympathy, sweat will get you change." How true that is. You must work at change. It doesn't just happen.

For many years I struggled with a short fuse, a bad temper. I used to excuse it as part of my genetic make-up. At times, I would call it my leadership temperament, until one day I had to face the awful truth: I just had a bad temper. I needed to change. I had to decide to deal with my temper, so I began a process of change. Rather than going off the handle, I had to learn to think of the consequences of my actions and words. The change required my consistent effort but I am better for it, and I am certain I have had many more opportunities, ones I might never have had, if I had let my temper issue go.

> *"Tears will get you sympathy, sweat will get you change."*
> *Rev. Jesse Jackson*

Our world has changed from an agricultural age to an industrial age, and now to an information age, yet many people still don't want to change with the times. I think it was Bob Dylan who sang, "The times they are a-changing. If you can't lend a hand, then get out of the way." Most people resist change because they don't understand it. Rosa McBeath-Canter of the Harvard Business School has said, "Individuals who will succeed and flourish will also be masters of change, adept at re-iterating their own and others' activities in untried directions to bring about high levels of achievement."

> "The times, they are a-changing. If you can't lend a hand, then get out of the way."
> Bob Dylan

When the local grocery store became the local supermarket, people reacted badly. They were worried. "How are we going to cope with this change?" they asked. "Who would want to go to the supermarket and pick their own food off a shelf?" Yet now we do it every day without thinking. Now we are seeing the change from the supermarket to e-commerce: the ordering of products and services on-line. If, like me, you are in your 40s, it might be a difficult concept, but for the average teenager and young adult, it's part of an every day process. Their world is a screen. They live there. The remote control epitomises their life – change is as easy as the push of a button.

Our world is changing – the television set can become a computer. Cell phones, only ten years ago the size of a brick and weighing about as much, are now the size of a hand, or smaller. From your cell-phone you can surf the internet, send and receive e-mail, and you can fax! It is possible to communicate almost in any way imaginable. You can even watch TV on some cell phones!

Things are changing. Be prepared and go with the flow of change. Don't fight change, welcome change. Don't resist change, embrace it, and adapt it into your life. Most people think to themselves, 'I won't change; I'll stay where I am.' However, the world continues to grow and expand, and if we stand still, rather than stay in the same place, we actually go backwards.

Globalisation is now a major part of our world. We have a global economy. We can't think of just our national economy any longer. Even a short 20 years ago few businesses really needed to pay attention to global markets – their national market was just fine. Today, from your own home, even from a plane flying, you can access your own personal business on a computer and work towards generating vast amounts of wealth. This is all a by-product of change.

I love change. I think change shows the 'bigness' of a person. In one of my fields of work, running a drug rehabilitation centre, one of my former staff members, and I underline the word former, came to me one day and said, "Why are we changing the program? We've done it the same way for the past 15 years." That's why he is a former employee. No-one can afford to do things the way they were done 15 years ago. I want to do things the way they're done today. Whilst we can learn from our past and adapt the good, we must also incorporate the newness of the now. Faith Popcorn was right when she said, "If you thought it yesterday, if you're thinking it today, you won't think it tomorrow."

The life story of musician Sonny Bono is one of positive change. Probably most well-known for his successful musical career, Sonny and Cher sold more than 40 million records. Sonny had borrowed $175 to record his first hit song. Sonny went on to television. *The Sonny and Cher Comedy Hour* was consistently in the ten-most-watched shows. Sonny then went into politics, first as mayor of Palm Springs and then in 1994 winning a seat in the House of Representatives. Sonny Bono didn't stay still, he changed with the times and with his circumstances. So can you.

> *"If you thought it yesterday, if you're thinking it today, you won't think it tomorrow."*
> *Faith Popcorn*

Change means better opportunities. One change makes way for the next, giving us the opportunity to grow. In 1928 Harry Cunningham worked in the stockroom of the Kresge Company. Harry was a good thinker and over the following years he was promoted. In 1957, as vice president of the company, he began to study the marketplace of the future. He concluded that discount stores would hold a major market share in the future. In 1959 he was appointed president and began the process of change that would see the establishment, in 1963, of 40 K-Mart stores. By 1977 there were over 1000 K-Mart stores throughout the United States. Today, you can shop at K-Mart throughout the world. Harry Cunningham saw the opportunity presented by the changing shopping habits of consumers. Rather than rejecting it, he capitalized on it and a successful international business was born. Someone once said "If we don't change, we don't grow; if we don't grow, we aren't really living." Discovering change is crucial to making the most of opportunity.

> *"If we don't change, we don't grow; if we don't grow, we aren't really living."*

President Ronald Reagan said of America, "The very key to our success has been our ability, foremost among nations, to preserve our lasting values by making change work for us, rather than against us." America has gone on to be this century's dominant economic, military and innovative force. It is living testimony to the fact that change can work for you.

CHAPTER NINE

Perseverance

I do not think there is any other quality so essential to success of any kind as the quality of perseverance, it overcomes almost everything, even nature.

J.D. Rockefeller

Finish What You Started

Many people in life are brilliant starters, but somehow they never finish. Any athlete will tell you it's not how you start the race that counts, but how you finish.

Often, people get off to a flying start in business, excited, full of expectations, full of great dreams, but some how they get side-tracked. It's like beginning to run a marathon, then, after a while, taking a detour and rather than getting back on track, staying on that detour until you end up somewhere you never really expected to be. It just doesn't make sense.

History is full of great starters, who ended up being not-so-great finishers. Sometimes, it's in the middle of our life race that we quit or fail to persevere or give up. It's not the beginning that counts. Although the beginning starts you off, you've got to continue to the end to make starting worthwhile. The important, indeed the most valuable, thing to do in life is to finish what you intended to do. How many great books will never be read because although they were started, they were left half written? There has never been a successful song left half written. Nor a successful business left only half built. The key is to finish what you started to do.

We have already talked about one of the greatest speakers of all time, Billy Graham. While Billy Graham and two of his peers, Chuck Templeton and Brian Clifford, started their race together, only one made it. What was the difference? Perseverance and commitment!

> *There has never been a successful song left half written. Nor a successful business left only half built. The key is to finish what you started to do.*

Many people with less talent, less ability and less enthusiasm achieve more than those with greater gifts because they have a commitment to end what they began to do. When someone enters a marriage, they don't enter it for a few weeks or a month or a few years, they enter it 'till death do us part'. They want it to end the way it started. And so it should be in business and in our personal endeavours. We've got to enter these opportunities with a mind to finish, to go all the way, not just part way.

It takes consistency to finish what you've started. Most people reaching the heights of success, whether financial or sporting, have been consistent. To get there, they have not been up and down like a yo-yo. They have built their lives consistently on the basics. They consistently try to go further. They consistently invest money. And over time, they do better than average, because they are consistent.

Just recently, I endeavoured a long run from my hometown, Sydney, to a neighbouring city, Wollongong, a distance of more than 120 kilometres. When I began to train, I would run with a young man who had spent many years training as a triathlete. From the beginning of our first training run, I tried to keep up with him, but to say the least, I didn't do too well. The next time, however, I found that if I ran consistently at my own pace, not shooting out of the starting blocks like a bullet, but steadily setting and maintaining my own pace, I did well and finished the race in a good time

You've heard the old story of the Tortoise and the Hare – slow and steady wins the race. Well I don't know about being slow, but what I would suggest is that we learn to be steady and consistent. Boxing legend Joe Frazier said, "It's the fighter that gets up in the early hours of the morning, and does the runs everyday, he gets up and takes no short cuts on the road. If you take a shortcut on the daily grind, it'll turn up under lights at night." You've got to be consistent if you want to make the most of your opportunity.

Perseverance is essential to achieving your dreams. The dictionary defines perseverance as "steady persistence in adhering to a course of action, a belief, or a purpose; steadfastness." Most people give up just when they are about to achieve success. They give up at the last minute, only moments away from winning their reward.

> "It's the fighter that gets up in the early hours of the morning, and does the runs every day, he gets up and takes no shortcuts on the road. If you take a shortcut on the daily grind, it'll turn up under lights at night."
> Joe Frazier

As I edged closer to the end of my run to Wollongong, the equivalent of three marathons over a period of two days, it was the last few miles and the last hill that was the most difficult. But unless I persevered through it and over that final hill, I would never have felt the thrill and exhilaration of knowing "I did it!" J.D. Rockefeller said this: "I do not think there is any other quality so essential to success of any kind as the quality of perseverance. It overcomes almost everything, even nature." My friends, how true that statement is.

Perseverance can overcome every single force, even

the critical tongue of the unsympathetic relative. It can overcome the limitations of a lack of education. It can overcome the boundaries in which other people try to fence us. It can overcome the sense of underachievement that we all struggle with. It's perseverance that sees us break through into a higher level of living.

Dennis Waitley and Reni L. Witt who coauthored *The Joy of Working* said this of perseverance, "It means giving full concentration and effort to whatever you are doing right now." What is it that you are doing right now? What opportunity have you been presented with, or are you involved in right now? Keep persevering on that. Keep pounding away until you strike oil.

> *"I do not think there is any quality so essential to success of any kind as the quality of perserverance. It overcomes almost everything, even nature."*
> *J. D. Rockefeller*

Clothing designer, Calvin Klein, loved fashion from an early age. For six years after graduating from a design course, he struggled to make ends meet. Just as he was considering leaving fashion altogether, to work in the grocery business, a friend gave him $10,000 to form Calvin Klein Ltd. Less than 10 years later, Klein had won three consecutive Coty awards. None of us know what success awaits our consistent perseverance.

Every human being goes through periods of discour

agement at some time or other. We all face it. The key is to break through it, and to realise that out of that discouragement, courage can come. Brian Tracy said, "Courage comes by acting courageously on a day-to-day basis." If you've faced discouragement, perhaps you will be surprised by those who have been there before you.

Henry Ford went bankrupt twice in his first three years in the automobile business. Three of Frank Woolworth's first five chain stores failed. Michelangelo lay on his back for seven years to paint the Sistine Chapel. Hewlett-Packard and Atari rejected innovative computer manufacturer, Apple. Twenty-three publishers rejected Dr. Seuss's first children's book. The 24th publisher sold six million copies!

> *Twenty-three publishers rejected Dr Seuss's first children's book. The 24th publisher sold six million copies!*

You may never become a brilliant history maker, a world class triathlete or a great inventor like Edison. You may never become famous like Madonna (thank God you won't!), but every one of us, if we take the opportunities presented to us, with a will to keep on persevering and a determination to succeed, can receive a measure of success that otherwise would have evaded us.

There is a brilliant story of a basketball coach attempting to motivate his players to persevere through a difficult season. Halfway through the season, he stood before his team and asked, "Did Michael Jordan ever quit?" The team responded, "No!" He yelled back, "What about the Wright brothers, did they ever give up?" "No!" the team resounded. "Did Wayne Gretzky ever quit?" Again the team yelled, "No!" "Did Elma Macalister ever quit?" There was a long silence. Finally one player was bold enough to ask, "Who's Elma Macalister, we never heard of him." The coach yelled back, "Of course you've never heard of him, he quit."

Planning helps you finish what you started. You've got to stick to your game plan. Understand that life and success must be planned. Why is it that most people spend more time planning their vacations than they do their success or their entire life? It's absurd that we can plan a one-week or two-week vacation, but devote so little time to planning our lives, mapping out a strategy to take us to where we want to be. It's the

> *Planning helps you finish what you started. You've got to stick to your game plan. Understand that life and success must be planned.*

planning and preparation that we put in to our success that matters. Champion NFL footballer, Roger Starbuck, said, "In business or in football it takes a lot of unspectacular preparation [planning] to produce spectacular results."

Now, take that big picture plan and break it into bite-sized pieces. In sports one game, one event, does not make a champion. It's a series of events, a series of victories, and also, most times, a series of losses that build the sporting champion.

> *"In business or in football it takes a lot of unspectacular preparation [planning] to produce spectacular results."*
> *Roger Starbuck*

Let me give you another example that might help illustrate this point. When you go to a smorgasbord restaurant, everything is laid out before you. Your eyes almost pop out of your head as you look at the salads, savouries, desserts, steaks, chicken, fries, and all the delicacies that will add incredible amounts of fat to your perfectly conditioned body! You want to try everything, but here's the point! You can't eat everything at once. Instead you've got to start bit by bit, piece by piece. At least that's how I approach a smorgasbord. (I often watch people pile everything onto one small plate.) I remember once going to a $10 all-you-can-eat buffet. My friend Sam had an incredible capacity to eat and he loaded his plate so full it was a miniature version of the leaning tower of Pisa! He sat down, with every imaginable and conceivable dish mixed together, looked at me and said, "Well Pat, there's a dollar's worth." He was determined to have that smorgasbord all on one plate ten times over. That's not the way you should approach life. You've got to take it piece by piece, portion by portion. You build a house one brick at a time. You build wealth a dollar at a time.

In September 1992, Mae Jamison became the first African-American woman in space. Few appreciated the persistence of her journey. Mae had been enthused by the fledgling 1960's TV series *Star Trek*. She graduated from college with degrees in chemical engineering, African-American history and medicine. Mae learnt three languages and served in the Peace Corp in Africa before she went into space aboard the space shuttle. Her persistence paid a great reward.

Most of us achieve so much, and yet give up because we don't feel good about where we're at, and we forget how far we've actually come. Management author, Fred Pryor, said, "One reason we don't attain our goals is we often focus on how far away we are from feeling satisfaction, rather than how far we've already come."

> *"One reason we don't attain our goals is we often focus on how far away we are from feeling satisfaction, rather than how far we've already come."*
> *Fred Pryor*

Helmut Schmidt put it this way, "It must be borne in mind that the tragedy of life doesn't lie in not reaching your goal, the tragedy lies in having no goal to reach." It isn't a calamity to die with dreams unfulfilled, but it is a calamity not to dream. It isn't a disgrace not to reach the stars, but it is a disgrace to have no stars to reach for. Not failure, but low aim is sin.

With opportunities, we've got to aim high, plan and then take the ground piece by piece!

Also by Pat Mesiti

MINISTRY TAPE SERIES

Who's Ruling Who

Have you been distracted from your destiny? It can be easy to lose sight of the goal, forget the prize and get sidetracked from fulfilling your ultimate destiny. In *Who's Ruling Who*, Pat gives a vibrant message on overcoming distraction. Some people are running towards things and some from things - which one are you? Pat shares that it's not how we start the race but how we finish that counts. Are you confused about whose report to believe? The spoken word can be a powerful ally or a devastating enemy. In *Who's Ruling Who* you will hear Pat give a triumphant message on harnessing the power of your tongue. AU$19.95 • CODE: TWRW

Soul Search: Soul Winning by Design

"He who wins souls is wise" Proverbs 11:30. In this inspiring new tape series Pat gives three powerful messages that have resulted in thousands of changed lives across the world. Nothing excites Pat more than seeing people come to Christ. Be encouraged and equipped as you listen to his classic message about life beyond the grave; his passionate call for the Church to change our generation through action and not only words; and his challenge for us never to be the same after an encounter with the cross. AU$19.95 • CODE: TSS

MINISTRY TAPE SERIES

His Earth His Wind His Fire

Time waits for no man. Now is our appointed hour. It's time to seek the Lord. It's time for revival. It's time to see people saved. It's time to take back what is rightfully the Lord's. It's time to redeem the time.
AU$19.95 • CODE: TEWF

Straight From The Heart

Pat will help you gain insight into those unexpected events in our lives that distract us from following God. You will discover afresh the proven principles of Christian living.
AU$19.95 • CODE: TSFTH

MINISTRY TAPE SERIES

Arresting God's Attention

God has always used hungry individuals who are willing to believe Him and dare to be different. This tape series will help you discover the power of one act of obedience. One message can change your life - this could be that message.

AU$19.95 • CODE: TAGA

The Power to Get Wealth

It's a fact that there is no shortage of money on Planet Earth. Who's got it? How do I get it? Where do I get it? How do I receive it, multiply it, and use it? In this tape series Pat addresses all of the above, plus much more! Get ready to receive inspirational and practical teaching on the life-changing principles of giving, investing & reward.

AU$29.95 • CODE: TPTGW

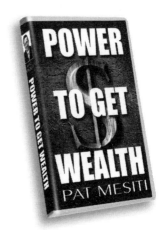

MINISTRY TAPE SERIES

Worship and the Word - Double CD

For the first time, the well-loved songs from Hillsong Music Australia are combined with the teaching of Pat and his friends, Pastors Brian Houston and Darlene Zschech. This double CD set features 10 songs and three messages: "This Is Your Day", "Obedience" and "The Lord Makes A Difference".
AU$39.95 • CODE: CDW&W

The Power of Obedience

This tape series is a biblical perspective dealing with the hidden things in our lives. Have you ever had sin or habit or struggle that no one knew about but you? Maybe you've dismissed it as a little thing yet you know within you that it is not meant to be part of your life and destiny. This message will help you overcome and propel you into God's plan for your life.
AU$19.95 • CODE: TPOO

BUSINESS TAPE SERIES

Super Success Strategies

How do you know when you have attained success? In this three tape power-packed series, Pat speaks on three major success strategies that will not only help you achieve success in the full sense of the word but help you to help others succeed.

AU$24.95 • CODE: TSSS

A - Z of Success

In this unique series, Pat Mesiti will help you to discover the principles that are necessary to fulfil your potential and secure your dream. One of the greatest fallacies that is common to man is that we think we know it all and yet as time goes on we realise we didn't know as much as we thought! Life is a journey - not an event. This tape series is not only visionary but also very practical and will provide you with the essential keys to developing all areas of your life.

AU$24.95 • CODE: TA2Z

BUSINESS TAPE SERIES

Wake Up and Dream

Vision and destiny are two essential ingredients for success in life. This series will cause you to wake up to the potential that you have and help you fulfil the dreams and destiny that we were all born to achieve. The world needs dreamers. It is your turn to be one.

AU$24.95 • CODE: TWUD

Building Big People

Business is about people, and people help build your business. This series will help you build big people without stepping on them. It will inspire you to inspire them to success in life.

AU$14.95 • CODE: TBBP

BUSINESS TAPE SERIES

Vision, Values and Destiny

How does someone find their destiny? In this tape series you will learn how to have a vision for your life and to help others reach their potential. Also how to define what destiny is and how to be a person whose business and ethical life is based on a solid foundation of good values.
AU$29.95 • CODE: TVVD

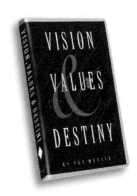

Better Than Your Best

This series will allow you to discover what it means to be a visionary and challenge you to change your mindset so that you can go beyond the "norm" and not settle for your current goal. Pat will inspire you to dream big!
AU$29.95 • CODE: TBTYB

The Winners' Circle

This three-part series will inspire you to overcome obstacles and pursue success. Pat is no stranger to adversity - his personal testimony is included. Come join the Winners' Circle!
AU$24.95 • CODE: TWC

BOOKS

Dreamers Never Sleep

This book will help you pursue your dreams. Pat, in his comical yet challenging way, will show you how to: replace wrong perceptions with winning attitudes, deal positively with change, define your destiny, go beyond the 'norm', handle failure and discover what success really is and how it can affect your world.
AU$16.95 • CODE: BDNS

Attitudes and Altitudes

Pat at his best. This book addresses the how's of leadership. It deals with vital principles such as leader development, how to network people and how to bring out the best in those around you. The wisdom, encouragement and practical teaching of this book will help you network and lead people into the 21st century.
AU$16.95 • CODE: BA&A

Wake Up and Dream

Discover the power of personal vision and how your dreams can change the world. The various topics include: how to rise above the limitations of your past, defining your dream, developing a plan to make your dream a reality, developing character, skills and attitudes that facilitate change, and unlocking the gifts and talents of those around you.
AU$16.95 • CODE: BWUD

Please rush me the following resources:

Books

❏ Attitudes and Altitudes   AU$16.95 (CODE: BA&A)
❏ Wake Up and Dream   AU$16.95 (CODE: BWUD)
❏ Dreamers Never Sleep   AU$16.95 (CODE: BDNS)
❏ Opportunity Knocks   AU$16.95 (CODE: BOK)

Ministry Tape Series

❏ Who's Ruling Who?   AU$19.95 (CODE: TWRW)
❏ Soul Search   AU$19.95 (CODE: TSS)
❏ His Earth His Wind His Fire AU$19.95 (CODE: TEWF)
❏ Straight From The Heart   AU$19.95 (CODE: TSFTH)
❏ Arresting God's Attention   AU$19.95 (CODE: TAGA)
❏ The Power to Get Wealth   AU$29.95 (CODE: TPTGW)
❏ Worship and the Word
Double CD   AU$39.95 (CODE: CDW&W)
❏ The Power of Obedience   AU$19.95 (CODE: TPOO)

Business Tape Series

❏ Super Success Strategies   AU$24.95 (CODE: TSSS)
❏ A - Z of Success   AU$24.95 (CODE: TA2Z)
❏ Wake Up and Dream   AU$24.95 (CODE: TWUD)
❏ Building Big People   AU$14.95 (CODE: TBBP)
❏ Vision, Values and Destiny AU$29.95 (CODE: TVVD)
❏ Better Than Your Best   AU$29.95 (CODE: TBTYB)
❏ The Winners' Circle   AU$24.95 (CODE: TWC)

Australian orders add 10% GST
Plus 20% postage TOTAL VALUE AU$ _____

Name _____
Address _____
_____
Ph (____) _____
Fax (____) _____
Email _____

Please debit my credit card to the value of AU$ _____

Type of card ❏ Master Card ❏ Visa ❏ Bankcard

❏ ❏ ❏ ❏ ❏ ❏ ❏ ❏ ❏ ❏ ❏ ❏ ❏ ❏ ❏ ❏

Expiry date _____

Signature _____

PHONE, FAX OR MAIL YOUR ORDER TODAY TO:

Pat Mesiti Ministries Inc.
PO Box 6873 Baulkham Hills BC NSW 2153
Ph: +61-2-9634 8800
Fax: +61-2-9634 8811
Email: pat@mesiti.com
Website: www.mesiti.com

For further information on other books and
resource material by Pat Mesiti look up
www.mesiti.com
or email: **pat@mesiti.com.**

You can also write to:
Pat Mesiti Ministries
PO Box 6873
Baulkham Hills Business Centre NSW
Australia 2153